CHANGE

*How To Turn Uncertainty
Into Opportunity*

by

Curtis Bateman
Marché Pleshette
Andy Cindrich
Christi Phillips, PhD

 FranklinCovey

Cover Design: Roberto Núñez
Cover illustration: Lauren Ball
Layout, Design and Illustration: Lauren Ball

For permission requests, please contact the publisher at:
Mango Publishing Group
2850 S Douglas Road, 4th Floor
Coral Gables, FL 33134 USA
info@mango.bz

For special orders, quantity sales, course adoptions and corporate sales, please email the publisher at sales@mango.bz. For trade and wholesale sales, please contact Ingram Publisher Services at customer.service@ingramcontent.com or +1.800.509.4887.

Change: How To Turn Uncertainty Into Opportunity

Library of Congress Cataloging-in-Publication number: 2022950390
ISBN: (print) 978-1-64250-794-2, (ebook) 978-1-64250-795-9
BISAC category code BUS106000, BUSINESS & ECONOMICS / Mentoring & Coaching

Printed in the United States of America

Contents

CHAPTER THREE

How We Experience Change 43

CHAPTER FOUR

The Mindset to Lead Change 63

CHAPTER FIVE

The Zone of Status Quo 81

Foreword

When I was a salesperson just starting out in my career, I serendipitously overheard Andy Cindrich, a coauthor of the book you're about to read, facilitating a strategy-execution session in the conference room next to my office. He said:

> "Here's the challenge leaders have. They've been thinking about a strategic decision for months before they breathe a word of it to anyone outside their core leadership team. They've looked at the data and the numbers, they've hashed out the risks and benefits, and they've gotten themselves to the point where they're willing to bet a lot on it.
>
> "Then they call their team or company together and announce the change. They're passionate about it, they're excited about it, and they might even communicate it effectively in the moment. They leave that presentation thinking, 'We're on our way!'
>
> "Then they metaphorically board a plane to fly to their next meeting, and when they reach cruising altitude going six hundred miles per hour, they look out their window and can't believe how slowly people on the ground are moving. And when the leader lands, they immediately fire off emails, saying, 'This is going to take the organization in an entirely new direction—what's the problem?'
>
> "What the leader failed to realize is that the people on the ground were tethered to that plane and were also moving six hundred miles an hour, colliding with each other, trying to adjust to the new speed, and struggling to balance what they used to do with what they now need to do. And that's hard work!"

As Andy taught, you can develop a strategy that looks perfect on paper, but sooner or later, you will be confronted with the responses and emotions of the actual human beings who will implement that change.

Two decades later, when I was serving as president of FranklinCovey, we lived out this phenomenon as an organization. In our case, the change was the result of a proactive decision to upend our business model and undertake a massive digital transformation. Things weren't going poorly for us; in fact, we were already doing better as an organization than we'd done in a long time. But our prescient CEO at the time, Bob Whitman, believed there was a better way to serve our customers: by transitioning to a digital-first subscription model. And if that proved to be true, it was going to be much better for our clients and our organization—including our people.

I was tasked with testing out the model with a subset of salespeople and clients, and results quickly proved the idea viable. But it was not an easy decision, as a public company, to transform our business. We needed to address literally everything: what we sold, the way we sold, the way we engaged clients, the financial model of the company, how we recognized revenue, how we accounted for our sales, how we went to market... in one way or another, it all had to change!

As we tackled those challenges, we knew that if we couldn't capture the hearts and minds of the people, the change would fail. Our job as leaders was to help everyone in the organization see that while we didn't have answers to every question, ultimately this was going to be the right thing for them and for our customers.

This is the very leadership challenge Andy was describing! Whether you're rolling out a strategic initiative or dealing with an externally imposed crisis, it's easy to forget that it's going to take your people more than one meeting or one presentation to get to the same level of comfort, buy-in, and excitement that you, as the leader, have for what's about to happen.

We often think leadership is about having the "big idea." But the idea is just the starting line. Leaders need a willingness to confront reality, adjust, get input, adjust again, and bring people along. That's the real work of leadership.

During our own change initiative, we were no exception. Some of the most influential opinion leaders in the company said, "I don't want to do this. I've been successfully doing my job for two decades, and you're going to come in and mess all that up?" (I know because they called me directly!) As an organization, we were in and out of what this book calls the Zone of Disruption frequently—sometimes multiple times a day. At the same time, we benefited from having a culture filled with incredible people who were already steeped in the principles and practices of resilience, trust, and collaboration from *The 7 Habits of Highly Effective People, The Speed of Trust*, and other bodies of work that are central to what we bring to the world. As a result, our cultural strength gave us a leg up on the change, and we pushed through to the Zone of Innovation relatively quickly—and the benefits of the change began to materialize.

We had all kinds of fits and starts and, thankfully, our clients hung in there with us. Our people recalibrated and innovated in ways we couldn't have foreseen at the beginning. Most importantly, our clients, people, and investors were truly better served as we began to form deeper and longer-term partnerships with our clients and engage with them in more lasting and comprehensive ways.

So why FranklinCovey and why this book? Why listen to us after the millions of gallons of ink that have already been spilled on the topic of leadership and organizational change?

Fundamentally, it's because we believe that we have a unique understanding of the underlying principles, practices, and behaviors that drive effective behavior change at scale—and we know how to enable organizations to marshal all that human energy to get aligned and rolling in the same direction in support of the strategies the organization needs to achieve. This is something we've been doing for forty years. We are the behavior-change company. And at its core, every strategic initiative, every change you go through, is accomplished through a change in human behavior.

We're checking the box that you've come up with a brilliant plan—whether it's to achieve better results or to deal with a change you never asked for. But that great plan will live or die based on what the people in your organization or team do. Whether they buy in or not. Whether they go on the journey or not. Whether they reinvent themselves and the way they work to make it happen... or not. As my friend Andy pointed out, having a great idea puts you at the starting line. The real work of leadership is what you do next.

Paul Walker
CEO, FranklinCovey
April 2023

Introduction

When Mick Jagger opened the door, Charlie Watts, the Rolling Stones' drummer, punched him in the face so hard he fell flat on the table behind him. The usually mild-mannered Watts then calmly turned around and walked back to his hotel room.

Why such an act of aggression? Jagger may have been one of the greatest rock and roll front men of all time, but he miscalculated the emotions of change. He hadn't learned (or had forgotten) that unwanted and unexpected change can tap into our most primal fight-or-flight instincts. Even a calm, unflappable English drummer could lash out—and did—when the ego-driven Jagger announced he'd negotiated a huge deal for *himself* with a slew of solo albums to follow. That act of betrayal, followed by a late-night harassing phone call from Jagger, was more change than Charlie Watts could take. A knock at the door was followed by a right hook, and Jagger fell into a platter of smoked salmon and nearly out of the hotel window.[1]

Eventually, the Rolling Stones patched things up and continued their streak of best-selling hits. While we're not advocating Charlie Watts's choice in handling the situation, we recognize it would be a mistake to underestimate how humans are wired to react when faced with the threat of change. We've written this book to provide leaders with the mindsets, skillsets, and toolsets to lead their teams from simply reacting to change, to opting in and taking ownership of it. In the chapters to come, we'll present a framework for how change unfolds as a predictable process and how leaders can increase their team's capacity to both implement and leverage the benefits of change. After all, FranklinCovey's mission of *enabling greatness in people and organizations everywhere* is essentially a mission about change. Whether we're developing exceptional leaders, instilling the habits of effectiveness, building an inclusive and high-trust culture, or providing a common execution framework tied to

"Wildly" Important Goals, change is at the heart of how people live, work, and achieve individual and collective "great purposes."

As four authors, we're unabashed about our passion for and expertise in helping clients successfully navigate change. It begins with a recognition that the most effective change leaders choose to invest their time in their people *over* following a process. Leaders who begin with this mindset can more easily move beyond rote change-management practices to building increased change capabilities in those they lead.

> *The most effective change leaders choose to invest their time in their people **over** following a process.*

Over the past four decades, we've vetted our framework by working in the trenches with executives, mid-level leaders, and frontline employees to support various forms of change across numerous industries. The topic of change has helped shape the focus of our professional lives, and we've gathered more than a few stories along the way.

Change Is a Platform for Helping Others

Curtis Bateman

It all began on a trip through Eastern Europe in the late '90s. I was working with one of our business partners, and we were discussing the need for individuals, organizations, and teams to have more tools and best practices when it came to change. We realized people needed a way to see the change journey like a map so they'd know where they were and what was ahead. With my business partners, I jumped to the whiteboard and sketched the initial vision for what later became FranklinCovey's Change Model (I know, nerd alert—who "jumps" to a whiteboard to draw a modified J curve?). Together, we sketched several years' worth of clients' successes and failures and teased out the common patterns that stalled or accelerated their progress during their change trajectories. What emerged over years of diligent study, reflection, and recalibration was a change model my experienced and talented coauthors and I will present and explore in this book.

Prior to our whiteboard "masterpiece," I'd spent the first dozen years of my career working in software and had the opportunity to collaborate with publishers all over the world. I was working at a boutique tech startup, and after landing our first big international client, I moved to Europe to ensure a successful implementation of our solution. We built a team of consultants, trainers, technical specialists, and salespeople. The software we sold to publishers became the backbone of their operations, including customer service, finance and revenue recognition, marketing, and fulfillment. Consulting with clients to implement our technology put me on the front row of large organizational change. Oh yeah, and very much on the front row of *personal* change as well, as my wife and I uprooted our family and moved halfway around the world. Best decision we ever made, and we've done it multiple times since.

In the ensuing twenty years, I've had the privilege of being involved in many significant change initiatives across complicated systems, technologies, and processes, and what I really learned is that change is fundamentally about... *people*.

This people-first insight eventually led me to the world's most trusted leadership company, FranklinCovey. I saw an opportunity to move our experience and ongoing change work into an organization with a much bigger stage—one with the potential to help everyone find more success with change. And that's a *why* that drives me to this day.

Change Promotes Growth

Marché Pleshette

One of my favorite adages in life is "Stop looking at your past... it's not where you're headed."

I've always felt a bit uncomfortable, and sometimes even paralyzed, at the onset of change, until I first gain clarity about why I'm in it; second, understand what I can and can't control about it; and third, make clear decisions about how I will move forward. What I've found over time is that I'm rarely guaranteed success at the outset of a new venture. But I've learned that success in any undertaking is far more promising when there's a planned process, a support system, and a focused and positive mindset for the journey.

My passion for people led me to the most fitting careers—professional development and personal coaching. They have given me the opportunity to support others in growth, improvement, and the accomplishment of goals. For someone who was so resistant to change personally, it's ironic that I found myself essentially in the business of change. In the most rewarding way, my career has not only helped others, but also helped me to consistently grow, improve, and reach higher goals myself.

While crisscrossing the world for several decades, working with FranklinCovey's diverse client base, I've become certain that change is a process of adjusting to something different or new and causes many of us to be fearful. And that's normal for all of us at some level. It's when fear hijacks our confidence and paralyzes our individual momentum that the potential upside of change falls short. This book is designed to help you, as a leader, guide your team past such fear and embrace the opportunities that await.

My greatest change, personally, came when I was twenty-four and I lost my father to a fatal car accident. I saw my dad, as many daughters do, as the greatest. He was such a source of wisdom, provision, encouragement, thoughtful conversation, and joy. I counted on him for almost everything! He taught me about life, business, and greatness, but I wasn't deeply listening to the responsibility part of our conversations, because I subconsciously thought he'd be there all my life.

The first several months without him were empty—emptier and more hopeless than I'd ever experienced. While going through the grieving process, I had to decide to accept both the loss and the opportunity to grow. I took on the things he'd originally done for me, often having no idea what I was doing with some of the business matters... but I learned. I became more self-sufficient and wiser in handling personal issues as well. Where I would ordinarily have called him to ask advice about a relationship or a big decision, I began to test the wisdom of my own insights and move through the natural fear of this massive loss in my life. I became more independent and found I was far more capable than I'd imagined I could be. The comfort of his presence in my life had created such a safe space, I hadn't leaned into the potential of my full growth. I would rather have had a different kind of growth spurt than losing my dad, but it was a pivotal point of enlightenment for me about change. Even now, I still miss him; but he would be so proud of the empowered and mature woman I've become.

Among those of my brilliant coauthors, my voice throughout the book is one that reminds us of the human spirit that is so much a part of change. Whether our change is personal, professional, organizational, or societal, it's our sense of self, our identity, our character that gets refined through the change process.

Andy Cindrich

Change Can Spur Greatness

As a twenty-nine-year-old high school principal with some staff who had taught longer than I had been alive, I led an amazing group of teachers, coaches, and students in turning our struggling school around. In just a three-year period, we were able to change the culture, improve academic performance, and establish winning traditions in several sports. At the outset, I knew I had to shake things up—people were too comfortable with the way things had always been at the school. We disrupted everything from the bell schedule and homecoming traditions to the way we collected gate receipts at football games and how the staff interacted with students. I also helped two teachers find opportunities more suited to their skillsets. That didn't sit well with the teachers union, who ultimately pressured the school board to move me out (known to the rest of the world as getting sacked). They didn't fire me outright but moved me into a new role where I split my time between two school districts, serving as the school community-resource director before moving back into the classroom and working with at-risk students. A reduction in force in the spring of my fifth year left me with a newborn baby, with a house under construction, and without a job too late in the year to find another as a school administrator, so I had to reinvent myself—*fast!*

I pivoted to instructional design, training development, editing, and even web development and search-engine optimization. My biggest client was FranklinCovey, and after a series of serendipitous events, I ended up as a full-time FranklinCovey consultant, helping clients with strategy execution, leadership development, and personal effectiveness. This gut-wrenching, unanticipated, and unwanted change is one of the best things that ever happened to me.

In my three-thousand-plus days of engagements as a Franklin-Covey consultant, I've seen the pain of people who get stuck—whether from a new boss, the grief that follows the untimely death of a loved one, a faith crisis, the bitterness of divorce, an empty nest, or the struggle of navigating organizational change. I've seen my children's friends get stuck after high school graduation, and I've seen clients get stuck when unanticipated change throws them off their game plans.

If you've noticed a theme, it's getting "stuck." Organizations and smart, well-educated, talented leaders and individual contributors all get stuck in change. My personal mission calls me to help people get *unstuck*, to reinvent themselves in the face of adversity, and to find their own greatness. This often means experiencing unanticipated value and joy from change. I recognize that change is essential to progress—whether as an individual, in a marriage or partnership, in business, in school, as a community, as a society, or even collectively as stewards of this world.

Change Is Universal and Predictable

Christi Phillips

Change is probably the main theme of my personal life, and it very easily has become a theme of my professional life. When I was eight years old, my parents came to me and my siblings and told us that they were moving our family to Africa from Texas. But before we got to Zaire (now the Democratic Republic of Congo), we had to move to Georgia for six months, then France for another six months. I didn't like any of that, but it didn't matter—it all happened anyway.

I eventually came to love moving from one place to another, and even missed the changes when my family settled back in Texas. Change, in the form of living in unfamiliar places, had opened me to new people, new learnings, and new paradigms. I eventually learned that I could choose to embrace such change or resist. I believe this insight gave me an edge that other people my age, without the benefit of such drastic and early change in their lives, simply didn't have.

For the last fifteen years of my professional life, I have functioned as a change agent, both formally and informally. I helped lead a large healthcare organization through the implementation of an electronic medical records (EMR) system—an experience both delightful and hard. I also took ten long years to complete a dissertation on employee engagement. It, too, was a change experience filled with both joy and pain.

Shortly, Curtis is going to introduce you to a parable about a ship, its crew, and their perilous river journey. When it comes to change, the waterfall in this parable represents the initial disruption of change. We stress the inevitability of plunging over the river's edge—whether accidental, imposed, or chosen—just as I was taken over such a change waterfall early in my life. As a reader, you may find that the waterfall and resulting journey works for you as a metaphor, particularly if you can envision a change story as a fantastical adventure. Or the whimsical waterfall may be difficult or challenging, if you prefer more literal translations of hard-hitting business-like change. The thing that is common about the parable you'll find in Chapter One is that, for nearly all of us, it represents the emotional plummet and heightened chaos, personal or professional, slight or significant, that change brings. My goal in giving you this early spoiler is to set you up, regardless of which kind of literary preferences you have or what kind of reader you are, so you can, in the best tradition of any useful parable, ascribe to the waterfall the meaning that flows from your life, experiences, culture, context, and more. In other words, make it yours.

This book emphasizes the people side of change, which, thanks to the work on grief—the emotional reactions to loss (certainly a kind of change)—presented by Elisabeth Kübler-Ross in the 1980s,[2] we understand is universal and predictable. I know that FranklinCovey isn't the first player in the sandbox to talk about the people side of change, but we've built upon that foundation to offer a simple and relatable model to reconceptualize how to self-manage, to take others through change, and maybe even learn to enjoy the ride.

We've each come to change through a different lens: Curtis as a change expert with over two decades of working both at the highest levels and in the trenches; Marché as a professional-development consultant who has coached hundreds of leaders through personal and professional change; Andy as a leadership and effectiveness expert and an accomplished change practitioner who provides consulting services to executives and organizations; and Christi as a PhD in human resources development who has served as the lead change agent for an immensely complex healthcare change initiative, among other change-related projects. We've experienced change from many perspectives, across diverse organizations, and from all parts of the globe, and our collective experience has validated two premises we'll explore further in this book:

- Change follows a pattern, and leaders can benefit greatly from a framework we call the Change Model.
- Because change is always a human endeavor, the most effective change leaders prioritize the needs of their people over strict adherence to a process.

The promise of this book is that it will teach you, as a leader, how to turn the uncertainty of change into opportunity (and build your team's capacity to move through current and future changes more effectively). That may feel like a daunting challenge, especially if you're in the middle of a change disruption. But take heart. The perfect antidote to change's complexity is a model that is clear and simple to understand. And so, by way of introduction, let's start with our parable...

CHAPTER ONE

Who Rocked the Boat?
(A Change Parable)

Wait... What? A Parable?

Curtis Bateman

As Christi mentioned in her introduction, we're going to start with a parable about a boat and its crew on a fantastical journey—one that forces them to adapt through disruptive change.

This story was previously released as an illustrated book titled *Who Rocked the Boat? A Story about Navigating the Inevitability of Change.* We've included the story here to unpack and explore it through the lens of leadership. We strongly feel that it brings to life profound principles and practices that can change the trajectory of one's career, levels of contribution, legacy, or even an entire organization.

So why a parable? Let me quote from Howard Schwartz, the editor of a collection of nineteenth- and twentieth-century parables called *Imperial Messages:* "...the modern parable—like its predecessor the ancient scriptural parable—is a brief story infused with a moral dimension. Meaning does not lie exposed on the surface but, submerged, waits for the reader who has ears to hear the message...."[3] And that's our invitation to you—to consider your own change journey and consider what meaning you might find beneath the surface as you join our captain and crew on their voyage.

One last note: We gave the parable the somewhat ironic title of *Who Rocked the Boat?,* as this is often the first reaction in the face of unexpected change—*whose fault is this?!* This can be especially true for newer leaders and teams facing daunting change for the first time. So let's begin with a text exchange between such a leader and a mentor they trust.

A Leader's Dilemma...

Tuesday, 10:41

Help!

Company just announced a
BIG change. My team's right
in the middle of it all. Yikes!

I've never led a team
through this kind of a thing
before :(

Tuesday, 10:50

What do I do?

Where do I start?

Breathe... You've got this

Tuesday, 11:23

Easy for you to say! I am so overwhelmed

I'm glad you messaged. This is why you asked me to be your mentor. Moments like this, right?

Right

Advice

I just sent you a whimsical story about change. Read it then text me when you're done

Part One

The River "Routine"

There once was a captain and crew who set off in their fanciful ship, *Results*. They had been tasked with delivering their cargo past the mountain where their port of call awaited. The crew was content, perhaps even a little bored, as *Results* moved at a slow but predictable pace.

Everyone expected a smooth journey—the waterway was gentle, the scenery pleasant, and the skies clear and comforting.

The crew had worked together for some time and knew each other well. *Move* was the engineer who kept their steam engine stoked and running. *Minimize* served as the chief mate and oversaw the cargo. *Resist*, the second mate, was responsible for ship and crew safety. *Wait* was a deckhand who did a little bit of everything. And finally, *Quits* and *Quit* were twins who took turns piloting the ship down the river. They all served under the captain, who was responsible for everything related to *Results* and her crew.

"I prefer gentle rivers like this one," *Wait* said to the others.

"They make for an easy trip," *Minimize* added.

"And it does give us time to run some drills," *Move* said, always an endless fountain of energy. "You know, sharpen our skills and learn something new!"

Resist raised an eyebrow in response. "Do more work for the same pay? Yeah, I'll take a pass."

"Same here," *Quits* called down from the helm. "Don't stress yourselves out—this trip will be as smooth as silk."

"True," *Quit* agreed. "Smooth as silk when I'm at the helm!" They all laughed at *Quit's* overconfidence.

But river journeys, like life, often unfold in surprising ways.

In the distance, the sound of a muffled roar rose above the chug of *Results's* steam-powered engines. Noticing the river moving faster and faster, the captain knew what it likely meant: waterfall ahead! But before they could swing the boat around, the swift current pulled them into a rushing, churning rapid.

"All hands, man the boat!" the captain exclaimed, issuing the traditional order for the crew to don their life jackets and prepare for the unknown. "Waterfall ahead!"

But not every crew member reacted in the same way.

Move, who loved the excitement of a new adventure, grabbed a shovel and began heaping coal into the boilers. "The quicker we get to the waterfall, the more exciting—and fast—our trip will be!" *Move* loved to race ahead and embrace the thrill of the ride.

Minimize, who wanted to know only what was expected and do as little as possible, was cautious not to overthink or expend more energy than necessary: "Is it really a waterfall? Let's not be doing any more than we have to," said *Minimize*, looking up from reviewing the cargo manifest.

Wait noted the captain's warning but remained in place. "I've been fooled by such noises before. Best to hold off and see what happens," *Wait* said, monitoring the rest of the crew and watching how they reacted before making a move.

Resist believed they should refuse to go further—a waterfall could easily destroy *Results*. *Resist* shouted to the others, "We must fight against the pull of the current! Help me throw the anchor overboard!" But the captain intervened—they were moving too fast, and if the anchor caught, it would capsize the ship.

Quits and *Quit* had other ideas. *Quits*, thinking the jungle a better alternative to the waterfall, shouted: "Good luck to you, but I'm outta here!" Then *Quits* jumped overboard and swam for shore.

Quit, on the other hand, wanted out but wasn't ready to abandon the ship or crew just yet. After all, who knew if the jungle was any less dangerous than the waterfall? So *Quit* stepped away from the helm, grabbed the rail, and said, "No use steering now."

The captain grabbed the wheel and guided *Results* toward the precipice ahead.

Part Two

Down the Waterfall

The ship bounced and listed as it neared the crest of the waterfall. Awash in the roar of the falls, the spray of the water, and the rush of the wind, the crew was gripped by an onslaught of emotions as they plummeted.

"I told you this would happen! We're goners!" *Quit* shouted above the fray.

"We should have dropped the anchor!" *Resist* exclaimed.

"Oh my!" *Wait* cried out, clinging to the rails and terrified of how much worse things could get.

Move whooped with delight and relished the adrenaline rush.

Minimize kept quiet.

The captain knew they were in the thick of it, and seeing emotions running high, thought, *How do I help the crew after we hit bottom?*

With a tremendous splash, *Results* plunged into the pool beneath the waterfall. The engines belched hot steam and shrieked in protest as the crew crashed and tumbled into each other. Several of the crew fell overboard, and others had to scramble to toss life preservers and pull them in. *Wait* was even forced beneath the water by the pressure of the falls but managed to swim back to the surface and be rescued. Drenched, battered, and hurting, the crew went on to assess the damage. *Results* had taken a significant beating, but the ship remained afloat as they drifted in the water's current.

"So now what?" *Resist* asked, prepared to oppose anything else that was new and unexpected.

Wait watched the others, looking for a clue as to what to do.

After assessing the ship's damage, the captain said, "The waterfall wreaked havoc on our poor ship and left us bruised and broken, and now we need to work together to get back on course."

"But why did we have to take *this* route?" *Quit* moaned. "There are lots of other waterways out there. Whose crazy idea was it to take the river with the waterfall?"

The captain replied, "If we were to always take the same rivers in the same ways, we'd never find faster and better routes. No river will ever stay constant, so waterfalls will always be a part of the journey."

"So, what now?" *Resist* demanded.

The captain offered a reassuring smile. "I know this is not what any of us expected, but we'll figure it out together."

"Couldn't agree more, Cap'," *Move* said enthusiastically. "Trying new things makes life more interesting."

"I don't need a more interesting life," *Resist* grumbled.

"For the record, I wanted none of this," *Quit* said. The current carried *Results* to a sandy beach where they dropped anchor and disembarked. As they gathered on the shore, they noticed how the sand pulled and tugged at their boots. It was slow-moving here, as if the place wanted to keep them stuck. The captain said, "I think we can rest here for a bit, but we don't want to stay too long. Let's decide what to do and get moving."

"As long as we don't spend too much time talking," *Move* said, shifting from foot to foot.

"Let's just find where the river picks up again *down here*," *Minimize* suggested.

"But that won't lead us to where we need to go," the captain replied. "Our charge is to take *Results* and her cargo to the mountains and port beyond—both of which are on higher ground."

"Well, the cargo can spoil for all I care," *Quit* said. "I hate it here."

"We still have a job to do," the captain said, looking up at the cliff. "That *hasn't* changed and getting to the top seems our best option."

"Okay then, sure... we'll just *magically* sail our ship up a vertical rock wall," *Resist* said sarcastically. *Resist* knew that sometimes the best way to stop an idea was to mock it.

Frustrated, the crew scattered to different points along the beach, lost in their own thoughts about what they were willing and wanting to do.

The captain approached *Wait,* who was sitting on a boulder. "Mind if I ask you something?"

Wait shrugged.

"Why is the team so hesitant to go up the cliff?" the captain asked.

"Well, I'd say the crew doesn't want to rush into anything."

The captain considered that for a moment and then asked, "Do you think that's true for everyone, or is it just how you're feeling?"

"Well, I know I feel that way. Plus, I've been through this kind of thing before, and it never works out. People can talk all the big ideas they like, but in the end, everyone just does their own thing."

Understanding *Wait's* concerns, the captain then had a similar discussion with each crew member. In the end, everyone had their own concerns and reactions, but what the crew mostly wanted was a clear, well-thought-out, and well-communicated plan that wouldn't end up being a waste of time. Following some intense brainstorming and discussion, the captain shared a proposal: "I think we should take the ship apart..."

"Hold on," *Resist* interrupted. "You're suggesting we take the *entire* ship apart? And then what...? Carry it up bit by bit? On our backs? That's the worst idea ever, Cap'. And no one here will ever support it."

But *Minimize* saw it differently. "It's really not such a big deal. We can construct a hoist using our pulleys, mast, and rigging, then pull *Results* up piece by piece. Better than on our backs, for sure. Of course, I'm not saying I *want* to go up the cliff, but if that's the plan, we can at least be smart about it."

"I love it!" *Move* exclaimed, to no one's surprise whatsoever.

"Have you forgotten how *much* it all weighs?" *Quit* asked. "Even if we break *Results* down to her smallest parts. I don't care how many pulleys we have; we'll never be able to do it." *Quit* then turned to *Resist*. "You're with me on this, right?"

Resist nodded with a dodgy grin.

"Okay," said the captain, "but what's the alternative?"

The crew glanced at each other. They couldn't think of a better way to get the ship and its cargo to the top.

The captain said, "Alright then. Let's get started." The others nodded in agreement, some less enthusiastically than others. But it was enough for *Wait* to see that things were happening. "I'll help you get the tools," *Wait* called out to *Move*, who had already taken off toward the ship.

The captain was pleased they had decided to get to work, and knew getting out of the ravine would stretch the crew in ways they weren't used to.

Part Three

Up the Other Side

The plan they came up with required several steps. First, they would break the ship down into manageable pieces. Next, they'd build ladders and scale the rock face, carrying the parts necessary to construct the winch at the top. Then, they'd use the winch to hoist the bundles and cargo. Finally, with everything and everyone safely gathered on the plateau above, they'd reassemble *Results* and put the ship into the river system—getting back to things just as they were before.

Everyone felt it was a solid plan, save for *Move*, who had left midway through the discussion and scaled a third of the cliff. *Move* had coils of rope, several pulleys, and an assortment of tools stuffed into a utility belt. The captain had to call *Move* back, who frowned but began the descent.

"You do realize we still need all that stuff down here!" *Minimize* shouted at *Move*, just so the point wasn't lost.

With *Move* back on the beach, the crew went about disassembling the ship, breaking down the steam-powered engine, unloading the cargo, unstitching and folding the canopy and emergency sails, coiling the ropes, securing the heavy pulley, and cutting the jigger mast to use as the arm for the winch.

Whenever a particular task felt daunting, *Minimize* reminded them they'd all been trained on ship repairs, so taking *Results* apart wasn't such a lofty endeavor. Eventually, the crew completed the breakdown of the ship, gathered the materials for the platforms, and built the required ladders.

Now it was time to climb.

But even *Minimize* had underestimated the required effort. It was extremely hard work. They had to find a suitable spot on the rock wall, hold the ladder in place, climb, secure it, build a small platform, then hand the next ladder up, repeating the process over and over. Sometimes the crew came to spots where they couldn't find any good places to fasten the ladder and had to back down and try a different route. Sometimes they had to lay the ladder sideways and travel in a direction they didn't want to go, hoping to find another way up. Other times, the wind threatened to blow them off the cliff! These and many more challenges had to be overcome as the crew zigzagged across the cliff's face, sometimes moving up, sometimes moving sideways, and sometimes moving down; but eventually and persistently, they continued the ascent.

Finally, they made it to the top. There they constructed the pulley as those below secured and hoisted the materials upward.

Success! Or so they thought.

It turned out, much to their dismay, that *Quit* had been right all along. The parts were too heavy, even with all their pulleys and the mast for support! Try as they might, the crew just couldn't muster enough strength to pull the heavy bundles up.

"You know that part of a story when you get to say, 'I told you so'?" *Quit* announced to the group.

"Please don't," *Wait* implored.

"Well, that was a waste," *Minimize* said, looking at the winch they had constructed.

"Couldn't disagree more," *Move* said. "We deserve some kudos for making it this far."

"Okay," *Resist* said. "Go ahead and give yourself a pat on the back. Feel better now?"

"*Move* does have a point," the captain said, knowing just how hard the crew had worked to get to where they were. "We solved all kinds of challenges on the cliff."

As the crew reflected on how hard they had worked, it did feel as if they had become better at figuring out how to overcome the unexpected.

"Remember when we were running low on bolts?" *Wait* asked. "We found a way to use the rock crevices as natural anchors."

"Or when the rock face jutted out and the ladders wouldn't work," *Move* said. "*Resist* made a *rope* ladder using a bunch of clever clove-hitch knots."

"It was the most efficient solution," *Resist* said.

Realizing all they had accomplished and with the captain's encouragement to try again, the crew shifted from complaining to solving the problem in front of them. Eventually, they decided they could repurpose the boilers and transform their people-powered winch into a steam-powered one. The boiler parts were big but not so heavy that the crew couldn't lift them on their own. That meant they could use their existing pulleys to get them to the top.

When they had finished hoisting the boiler parts, *Move* reassembled the components and adapted the steam engine to the new task.

When it was done, and the fire lit and stoked, the crew stood back and watched. Suddenly the piston began to move, then began pumping as the exhaust hiccuped puffs of steam. *Minimize* pulled the lever and their new, mechanical winch turned with ease. The crew shouted in celebration, giving each other high fives. The captain smiled, noting it had been some time since they had had a win like that. A very long time, in fact.

When all the ship's heavy cargo and large pieces were out of the ravine, the crew made their last climb, retrieving their ladders and platforms as they scrambled to the top. Up and down, over and over. Scaling the cliff had turned out to be even harder than the captain had predicted. But as long as the crew had worked together, step by step and foot by foot, they had gotten themselves out.

From their new vantage point, the captain and crew could see the waterfall and river that marked the beginning of their journey. And across the grassy highlands, they caught sight of a river leading to the mountains. Everyone was exhausted but proud of their accomplishment—soon they'd be back to the way things had been!

Part Four

The Sky's the Limit

But something was different.

The crew had changed. They began to celebrate.

"Say what you will, but we've overcome a lot to get to this point," the captain said. "And hey, it took everyone working together."

The captain then turned to each of the crew members in turn: "*Move*, you're never stuck in the old way of doing things. I can always count on you to try something new. And *Minimize*, I love how you always focus on what's necessary so we don't get in over our heads. *Wait*, you ask the best questions, and you don't rush headlong into things. *Resist*, you force us to test our thinking, which is invaluable. And *Quit*, even when you're disengaged, I've learned you can be an early warning signal to something the rest of us may not be seeing. What an amazing crew you are! It's great to be back on track, but we sure lost a lot of time."

Minimize said, "I don't want to be away from home any longer than we have to. Makes me wonder what *else* we could do to speed things up."

"That's an interesting thought," *Move* said.

"Maybe we should come up with some ideas," *Wait* suggested. "Like reassemble *Results* so it cuts through the water faster."

"Or leave some of the unnecessary cargo behind," *Quit* suggested, liking the idea of not having to move everything back to the vessel.

Move added, "I bet I could get more power out of the engines if I modified them more."

"A faster ship on a winding river is a terrible idea," *Resist* said, suspicious of any change that came with an overabundance of enthusiasm.

"I love the creativity," the captain said, "but *Resist* has a point—the river has some natural limitations. I wonder if there's a way to get *off* the river...?"

"What about a steam-powered walking machine?" *Move* suggested, liking the idea of stomping around in a giant mechanical rig.

"*Stepping* off a waterfall? Should I take the rest of the day to explain what a horrible idea *that* is?" *Resist* asked. "Because I could."

"Well, I don't see how *stepping* off a waterfall is any better than *floating* off of one," *Wait* replied.

"Wait a minute," *Resist* said flatly, "let's not get crazy. We're a *ship's* crew. That's what we know, and that's what we should return to."

"But there are different kinds of ships, aren't there?" *Move* said. "Different ships do different things and solve different problems."

Wait considered the idea for a moment then exclaimed, "Like *air*ships!"

The captain could suddenly see it and turned to the parts spread across the grass in ordered piles. "An *air*ship... it's not so impossible when you think about it. Same basic build, just some modifications to get us off the ground. Just think of it... in an airship, we could sail above the rivers and jungle at great speed—*Results* would literally rise!"

Minimize could envision it as well. "Still a ship, sure, but changed just enough to make it better. The canopy could be stitched into a balloon."

"Fine... it's a big modification, but it's not impossible. We have plenty of material, especially with the emergency sails."

"And the steam from the boilers could heat the air and give us lift," *Move* said. "We'd need a good deal for all the cargo, but those engines run hot."

"And the propeller could turn like before, only now in the air instead of the water!" *Wait* exclaimed. "Same basic mechanism as before."

"You'd need a helmsman to steer her," *Quit* said. "But that feels close enough to my job as before. Just... higher."

With renewed energy, the crew went to work turning their idea into a reality.

Sometime later, as the sun rested on the horizon, a new airship took shape. With its canopy and sails refashioned, boilers repurposed, and propellers realigned, the vessel rose into the air. The rudders, now serving as fins, turned as *Quit* spun the helm. The airship gracefully pivoted toward the mountains, the direction of their port of call. No longer were the captain and crew subject to the slow and meandering rivers that stretched out beneath them.

In the distance, the crew caught sight of *Quits*, who stood at the edge of the jungle and waved in astonishment. They could only hope *Quits's* next adventure would be as rewarding as theirs. But for them, in their new airship, the captain and crew steamed ahead with greater speed and efficiency than before. There would be challenges to come, of course, but those were for another time. Besides, the crew had learned they were more resilient and innovative than they had previously believed. And so in this moment, they celebrated the fact that where *Results* had once moved along a slow and mostly predictable path, she now soared.

As did they.

Wow. That waterfall is totally my life right now!! So many thoughts...

Where should I start? I have a gazillion questions

Easy! :)
Share the story with your team. Ask them to read it

I'll send some conversation starters. Pick some and start talking with your team

Thanks! That was fast

That will get you started

Lunch tomorrow? We can talk about how it went. Next steps

Sounds great. I'll review what you sent and we can talk then. And seriously, thanks!

CHAPTER TWO

Getting Started

W elcome back.

Now that we've spent some time with the captain and crew of the good ship *Results*, chances are their change story feels familiar in many ways to experiences you've had with change. Maybe your ship is teamed a little differently, your waterfall higher or lower, your cliff more gentle or jagged—but you've likely experienced a smooth start, a disruption, a decision, a climb, and an opportunity for more.

And let's be clear, as a leader, every time your team is at the bottom of the waterfall, it's creating cost for the organization—when your technology implementation falls short, when your new compensation model lands with a thud, when a new leader joins and relationships are strained—and you can add your last (or current) change to the list. Whatever that change happens to be, the faster you can lead your team out of the ravine, the faster those costs dissipate and even turn into new opportunities.

We'll be returning to *Who Rocked the Boat?* throughout the book. First, let's overlay our fictional story with one that almost sounds like fiction but is drawn from real life. Suspend your judgment, because although the story is true, you're going to frequently wonder how any of this could have happened in the last decade.

In 2012, a real estate investor closed on the purchase of an apartment complex. Unsurprisingly, the transaction came with a lot of paperwork. But this one came with one extra set of documents: a class-action lawsuit from the HOA of the property.

Why? Residents of the apartment couldn't get their pizzas delivered.

Now, this may sound like a trivial indictment, but there was more to it. The apartment building, which had no phone lines or cell service, was gated with a security system. Any visitor had to push an intercom button designed to connect to the nonexistent land lines. When the system was reconfigured to route to the residents' cell phones, this also didn't work, as none of the residents could get service from within. Consider some of the ramifications:

- The pizza-delivery person arrives. You don't know anyone's at the gate, and the pizza is subsequently returned and never eaten (at least by you).
- An online retailer delivers a package. That lava lamp you've been anxiously waiting for, which requires your signature, never finds a place on your bookshelf.
- Your date arrives to pick you up. They think you've stood them up, as you don't answer the intercom and your cell phone goes straight to voicemail.
- Your grandmother comes to visit. She's left wondering what kind of ungrateful grandchild allows an old woman to be left out in the cold.

Not great when it comes to receiving visitors and deliveries. But the lack of cell-phone service meant no *outbound* calls from the residents as well. Suffering a cardiac emergency? Do your best to crawl outside with your cell phone in hand and *then* dial emergency services.

Thus, the class-action lawsuit.[4]

That's the backstory; now, the change. Enter Adam Rubey and Chad Ballard, who specialized in high-end residential automation, lighting, and audio. Their investor client asked them to take on the challenge and solve the issue, even though this was far outside their expertise as they were used to configuring single-family homes but weren't familiar with this apartment's older (and useless) system. Adam and Chad chose to go over the waterfall and change what they did in their business.

First, they tried many of the available off-the-shelf products, but those failed. Then, they tried a few custom solutions, but nothing worked. After a good deal of trial and error and more than one setback, they eventually created their own solution, combining their engineering know-how with familiar hardware, and developed a configuration that worked. Success! Residents could now get their pizzas. They could call that date for a second chance. They could bring Grandma in out of the cold! Adam and Chad had saved the day, making the long climb up the cliff and out of the ravine. The residents were happy, the investor was happy, and no more lawsuit. End of story.

Or at least it could have been.

Adam and Chad made it to the top and they could have been satisfied with simply getting back to the way things had been. But instead—like *Minimize* in the parable, who said, "Makes me wonder what else we could do"—they grew curious. They contemplated whether owners of other commercial buildings faced similar problems and could use their newly acquired expertise. And it turned out, they could. Shortly thereafter, the company Illuminati Labs was born, specializing in making all kinds of commercial buildings cell-phone-friendly. Chad and Adam used their newly acquired "change muscle" to try something new—to be curious, to explore, to innovate. Like the crew in our parable, they found their *Results* took off in a new and exciting direction.

Such a positive outcome doesn't surprise us, since Chad and Adam replicated much of what made the captain and crew turn their change from uncertainty into opportunity. We'll explore this further by introducing the Five Common Reactions to Change and the Change Model.

The Five Common Reactions to Change

There are five common reactions to change:

* Move
* Minimize
* Wait
* Resist
* Quit/Quits

As you've likely noticed, those are the exact names of the crew members in our parable. And while it may be tempting to label these reactions as "good" or "bad," the reality is that each comes with its own strengths and weaknesses. There is no single "best" way to react to change—it's all about context. Even Quit/Quits is not an inherently wrong choice—some change

There is no single "best" way to react to change. It's all about context and choice. Each reaction may be right in any given context.

waterfalls plummet into shallow pools lined with jagged rocks, so jumping off the boat and swimming for shore can be the right call (although, in business, that's generally the exception and not the rule). It would be a mistake for leaders to view change as a black-and-white set of problems with a precise set of dos and don'ts to follow. The inherent complexity of change requires a thoughtful approach and a steady, skillful hand on the wheel.

Curtis Bateman

How We Identified the Five Common Reactions to Change

Over the many years I've consulted and worked with organizations, leaders, teams, and individuals on how to navigate change, I often found that people were surprised by others' reactions to change and didn't know what to do with their own. Leaders and their teams needed a way of talking through change; they needed a common language to communicate and understand each other.

So in our consulting, after we observed how people reacted to change, we identified common reactions and created a shared, nonthreatening language around these reactions—a language people can use to communicate safely how they feel about change.

Our primary lens in this book is focused on business organizations, but we have found that the common reactions to change can be observed in all kinds of contexts, including personal lives, families, sports, academics, the military, and many more.

Getting stuck in our own status quo can be as risky for us as anyone else.

Originally, we started with *Move*, *Minimize*, *Resist*, and *Wait*, but that was challenged some years ago when I was giving a keynote to five thousand people. I asked the audience to stand and engage in a change activity, only to notice a handful of people leaving the room.

They quit.

I realized that "walking out" and simply refusing to take part was another common reaction to change and something we hadn't included. Quitting can, and does, happen with regularity (the distinction between *Quit* and *Quits* is that one stays and refuses to engage, while the other leaves). This is happening with such regularity today that the term "quiet quitting" has become an increasing part of our vocabulary, with employees choosing to do the bare minimum, taking a step back from all emotional investment and engagement in their work. Even our self-initiated change efforts, undertaken with the best of intentions and wellspring of motivation, can find us throwing in the towel (ever quit a diet?). So *Quit* became one of our change reactions. And who knows? With more time, we may come up with another. We are in the change business, after all, and getting stuck in our own status quo can be as risky for us as anyone else.

Keep in mind that the Five Common Reactions to Change are *not* personality types. A personality type is a psychological classification or typology about a *person*. A change reaction is a *behavioral* descriptor—a momentary "snapshot" taken at any point in the change process. Our reactions to change are fluid, influenced not only by the change itself but our culture, team dynamics, community norms, institutional standards, and other considerations. They may be automatic, but learning to adapt and manage them is an essential change and leadership competency.

A Deeper Look at the Five Common Reactions to Change

Let's examine the Five Common Reactions to Change in more detail, considering the potential advantages and disadvantages of each.

Move

"Let's go!"
Move has an impulse to charge quickly into action toward the new objective.

ADVANTAGES	DISADVANTAGES
• Avoids getting stuck in old ways	• May act too quickly
• Tries new things (often eager to do so)	• Moves without getting "all the information"
• Stays motivated	
• Tolerates high levels of risk, ambiguity, and uncertainty	• Leaves others behind
	• Can lack credibility
• Energizes others	• Can be overly enthusiastic and emotional about change

Minimize

"Just tell me what you want me to do."
Minimize focuses on what's expected and tries to change as little as possible.

ADVANTAGES

- Focuses on what's necessary

- Avoids unnecessary disruption

- Tries new things to test them before fully committing

- Identifies efficient ways of getting things done

DISADVANTAGES

- Does little to change and subsequently gets little from it

- Has a lower commitment level

- Burdens the change efforts of others

- May be perceived as lazy

Wait

"Let me know when it's real."
Wait does nothing immediately. They hesitate for a variety of reasons, including watching to see what others do first, delaying until they have more information or options, or holding back while prioritizing other things first. They often have history on their side as they've seen numerous changes fail—they've been rewarded for not moving forward.

ADVANTAGES

- Avoids the downside of risk

- Often asks great questions about change

- Considers the change thoughtfully rather than rushing into it

- Conserves resources

- Not whipsawed by failed changes

DISADVANTAGES

- Misses the upside of risk

- Adopts change slowly and only after others have changed first

- Slows the adoption rate of others

- Misses opportunities that benefit from quick decisions

- Reacts to external events rather than being proactive

Resist

"Why are we doing this?"
Resist dislikes the change and tries to prevent it or convince others to fight it, privately or publicly.

ADVANTAGES

- Tests the rationale behind a change initiative

- Seeks alternatives

- Asks questions that reveal potential obstacles

- Counterbalances an overabundance of enthusiasm

- Sees the potential flaws in how others react to change

DISADVANTAGES

- Impedes progress

- Creates conflict and/or power struggles

- Raises invalid concerns that take time and energy to resolve

- Dampens morale and enthusiasm for the change

- Fuels fear and uncertainty

Quit

"I'm not doing that!"
Quit stays in the organization, the relationship, or the situation,
but gives up and refuses to engage with the change.

ADVANTAGES	DISADVANTAGES
• Offers an ongoing warning signal for potential obstacles	• Causes disruption and uncertainty
• Prompts leaders to provide better clarification and communication	• Creates drag on the organization and slows productivity
	• Actively undermines leadership
	• Negatively affects team morale and unity
	• Forces others to work that much harder

Quits

"I'm outta here!"
Quits is a variation of Quit. Quits leaves the team, relationship, or venture
because of a change, choosing to pursue something different.

ADVANTAGES	DISADVANTAGES
• Allows the leader to conserve resources	• Causes disruption and uncertainty
• Relieves the organization of a fence-sitter—they've made their choice	• Decreases the morale, unity, and productivity of the team they left behind
• On rare occasions, "abandon ship" can be the right call	• Costs the organization/team to find workarounds and/or a replacement
	• Forces others to work that much harder
	• Others may consider quitting as a viable option

Captain's Corner

Managing Your Reaction to Change

Throughout the subsequent chapters, you'll find "Captain's Corners" such as this. They are tactical leadership guides for assessing important aspects of change and leading your team through change conversations. As such, they've been highlighted for quick reference, and we encourage you to use them as you implement change initiatives with your team.

As you learn to manage your own reactions to change, you'll be able to model and coach your team to do the same. Share the following steps for when you catch yourself having an automatic reaction to an unexpected or unwanted change:

1. Pause and breathe.
2. Label what you are thinking and feeling.
3. Ask: Is this reaction helping me or preventing me from making progress?
4. Focus on what you can control, both about the change itself and how you choose to react to it.

The Change Model

When navigating change, leaders benefit from having a model, so teams can visualize where they are now, where they want to go, and whether they're making progress. No matter the source of the change—self-directed, environmentally forced, or organizationally initiated—the Change Model helps assess whether you have the ability and stamina to make the change and whether your efforts will pay off in a positive ROI.

The *Who Rocked the Boat?* parable places our model in a narrative form, representing the consistent and predictable change pattern people and organizations go through. We've tested the Change Model with "boots on the ground" inside organizations around the world and validated it as both a predictive and a diagnostic tool for change. We've also used and benefited from the Change Model time and time again in our personal lives.

Christi Phillips

Addressing the Need for a Change Model

A search for academic papers about change shows that nearly a million articles have been published in the last ten years. I have taught and implemented at least four change frameworks as a change practitioner and studied the bulk of them along my path to a PhD in human resources. I find that parts of such frameworks can be useful, especially understanding the emotional reactions to change (thank you, Elisabeth Kübler-Ross), and the need to identify defined steps (thank you, John Kotter), and learning to account for existing factors (thank you, McKinsey & Company). But the world of work is changing. As our work and social environments shift toward employing empathy and building agile teams and collaborative cultures, we need to understand what is happening with *people*, not just with change. This is where my friend Curtis Bateman started when building the Change Model.

Our model began with client conversations about what seemed to be a repetitive pattern of organizational change. This pattern was then tested with other clients: "Does this step make sense? Does it match your experience?" If a step matched the client's experience, that piece was locked. If they said no, then it was changed. Getting the Change Model firmed up took several years of trial and error. Over time, four distinct zones emerged that overlay the individual and organizational change journey. These zones created clarity for all audiences to locate where they were in the change process and then identify common reactions and actions that can improve change success.

Change requires that people take time to surface their own experiences and beliefs relative to the ongoing change. The best leaders intentionally guide their team members to help them figure that out and work through it—that's really the "management" part of change. But you don't need a weeklong certification course or a PhD to get good at this. Just keep reading. I think this Change Model—my new favorite—is the best yet...

Just as one's reaction to change is a momentary snapshot, the Change Model adds clarity at any given moment across a change initiative. We can further use it as a map to chart the way forward: anticipating key decisions, adopting new behaviors, and building a path toward innovation.

Time and Results

Consider the x (Time) and y (Results) axes that frame the model.

FIGURE 1: *X and Y Axes of the Change Model.*

The Change Model maps the results we get over time. It's tempting for leaders to see results as only financial, but they can include anything affected by change: morale, skills, confidence, productivity, engagement, time to market, health, leader-employee relationships, etc.

In the beginning, we experience a consistent, if not predictable, level of results. This was the River "Routine" in our parable, where the ship *Results* "moved at a slow but predictable pace. Everyone expected a smooth journey—the waterway was gentle, the scenery pleasant, and the skies clear and comforting."

FIGURE 2: *The River "Routine."*

Then a change is introduced, and results take a hit. "The ship bounced and listed as it neared the crest of the waterfall. Awash in the roar of the falls, the spray of the water, and the rush of the wind, the crew was gripped by an onslaught of emotions as they plummeted."

One of the leader's goals through change is to shorten the duration of the initial stress and limit its negative impact on results.

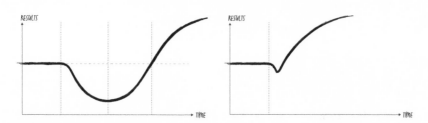

FIGURE 3: *Reducing the Depth and Duration of the Dip.*

Then there comes a time to decide to engage, when leaders and their teams commit to making the climb back to the level of results prior to the change. As our captain pointed out in *Who Rocked the Boat?*, "The waterfall wreaked havoc on our poor ship and left us bruised and broken, and now we need to work together to get back on course."

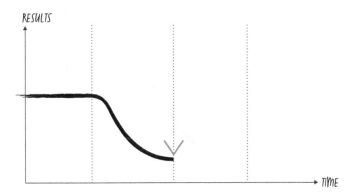

FIGURE 4: *Choosing to Engage in the Change.*

Climbing out is hard work and requires trying new things, enduring setbacks, and persisting in the effort. In the parable, the captain and crew found that "scaling the cliff had turned out to be even harder than the captain had predicted. But as long as the crew had worked together, step by step and foot by foot, they had gotten themselves out."

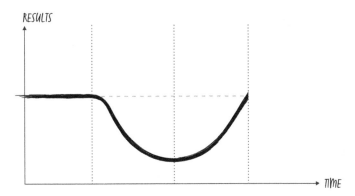

FIGURE 5: *Climbing Out.*

The change process can also result in a unique opportunity to innovate so that results climb even higher than before. In our parable, we describe it as,

"Sometime later, as the sun rested on the horizon, a new airship took shape. With its canopy and sails refashioned, boilers repurposed, and propellers realigned, the vessel rose into the air." The "rising into the air" was an intentional way of expressing *Results* literally taking off because of the captain and crew's curiosity and investment of energy and time.

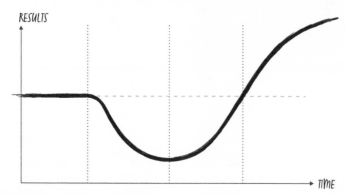

FIGURE 6: *Taking Off With Innovation.*

Many leaders try to pretend the dip doesn't exist. They think of their change as only up and to the right. Of course, sometimes serendipity happens and change yields immediate benefits. But it would be naïve to rely on such an outlier as an effective change strategy.

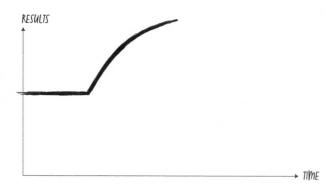

FIGURE 7: *Up and to the Right Is Rare.*

The Four Zones

Moving from the *x* and *y* axes of Time and Results, we next overlay the model with four distinct zones:

- The Zone of Status Quo
- The Zone of Disruption
- The Zone of Adoption
- The Zone of Innovation

CHANGE MODEL

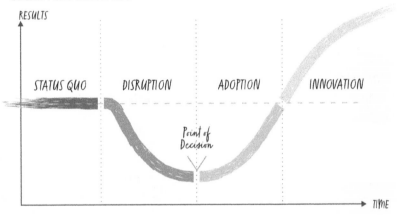

FIGURE 8: *The Change Model.*

In *Who Rocked the Boat?*, the four zones correlate with the status quo of the river, the disruption of the waterfall, climbing the cliff, and the adoption of new strategies through trial and error, with innovation—a new "airship"—at the end. Let's take a high-level look at each zone before going deeper in subsequent chapters.

The Zone of Status Quo (Chapter Five)

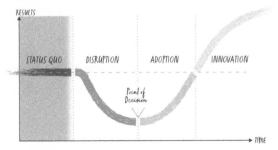

FIGURE 9: *The Zone of Status Quo.*

The Zone of Status Quo is what you experience before a change happens. Here, you are in a routine, and it's business as usual. Even if your routine is busy and stressful, it's still familiar. It can be difficult leaving the established behind.

Key Skill: Prepare

Those who are most successful at change prepare for it. They aren't content to try and avoid it or simply wait for it to happen. When change appears on the horizon—whether self-initiated or not—they can better navigate the impending disruption.

The Zone of Disruption (Chapter Six)

"The riskiest thing we can do is just maintain the status quo."
—*Bob Iger, American businessman and CEO of the Disney Corporation*

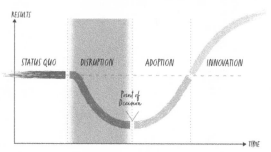

FIGURE 10: *The Zone of Disruption.*

As you plummet over the edge of the change waterfall, you enter the Zone of Disruption. Like the crew in our parable, it's easy to find yourself awash in chaos and ambiguity when results take a nosedive. Many of the things you were used to having can disappear, and what you were used to doing stops working.

Key Skill: Clarify

We can become stuck in the Zone of Disruption unless we clarify the impact of the change. Here we are concerned with three primary questions:

- *What's* changing?
- *Why* is it changing?

* *How* will it affect me?

Leaders can fight change insecurity with information, helping their teams commit to the change with greater confidence.

The Point of Decision (Chapter Seven)

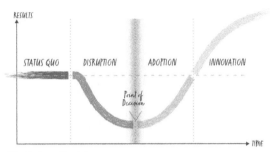

FIGURE 11: *The Point of Decision.*

The Point of Decision is a critical transition from the Zone of Disruption to the Zone of Adoption.

Key Skill: Commit

Here we use the clarity uncovered in the Zone of Disruption to commit to a choice: stay in the Zone of Disruption, with its lower results and lack of progress, or proactively own the change by taking action. We don't always get to choose whether a change happens to us, but we do get to choose how we'll respond.

The Zone of Adoption (Chapter Eight)

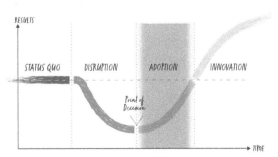

FIGURE 12: *The Zone of Adoption.*

The Zone of Adoption is where most change efforts die. But like the crew in our parable, you can learn new things as you make your way out of the dip.

Key Skill: Persist

In the Zone of Adoption, you're apt to get frustrated or be tempted to give up. Persistence is key as you scramble to the top, testing new tactics, learning from failures and setbacks, shifting your approach, and altering your thinking. It's this very struggle, as inefficient and painful as it may be, that lays the groundwork for future innovation.

The Zone of Innovation (Chapter Nine)

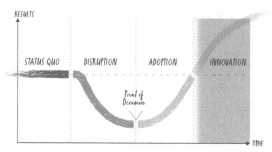

FIGURE 13: *The Zone of Innovation.*

The Zone of Innovation leverages the change experience you've earned so that new actions feel natural.

Key Skill: Explore

You've paid the price for innovation, and now you can leverage the investment on behalf of yourself and your team. In the Zone of Innovation, you explore new ways of thinking and doing, challenging assumptions and broadening your curiosity. Not all change needs or benefits from innovation, but one of the great benefits of change and following the model is taking stock of what could happen now that you've experienced new things, overcome significant challenges, and gained a new perspective on what you do.

Captain's Corner

Introducing the Change Model to Your Team

One of the first things you can do as a leader is introduce your team to the Change Model. Having a common metaphor and/or nomenclature helps ensures that everyone is "speaking the same language" when it comes to change. Once you've become familiar with the Change Model, there are several ways you can accomplish this:

- **Option One:** Hold a team meeting and set up a whiteboard (or build a visual presentation or other way of displaying the model). Use the content in this chapter to provide an overview of each zone.

- **Option Two:** Read the *Who Rocked the Boat?* parable in Chapter One aloud as a team.
  - Help your team understand and identify with the Five Common Reactions to Change. Keep in mind that each bullet is worthy of exploration and discussion. Don't feel pressure to move through each bullet as quickly as possible. Take the time to unpack this with your team and help them focus on their own reactions, rather than those of others.
  - Ask each team member:
    - Which one are you? Are you introspective around your own change reaction or aware of the reactions of others: Move, Minimize, Wait, Resist, Quit/Quits?
    - Could you empathize with some of the crew more than others? Who felt most like you?
      - ∞ How is your reaction helping you make progress?
      - ∞ How is your reaction preventing you from progressing?
      - ∞ How can you choose to react differently if it's holding you back?
    - How did the relationships between the captain and the crew come to make the change successful (or undermine its chances for success)?
    - Reactions to change can extend beyond the five most common reactions in the parable. What other reaction might represent you or someone you know when going through change? (Examples: Revolt,

who's ready to grab a torch and metaphorically burn the initiative to the ground; Fear, who is gripped by negative thinking and dread and will share it at every opportunity; Ambivalence, who is uncertain or unable to decide what course to follow; etc.)

♦ After exploring your team's reactions to change through the parable, use Option One to show how the parable follows the Change Model, and let your team know you'll be having more discussions about your current change in the days to come.

• **Option Three:** If you have the resources and interest to do so, purchase the stand-alone *Who Rocked the Boat?* book for members of your team. Invite them to read it independently and come to a team meeting to discuss how it applies to them individually, to the team, and to the organization. Because the book also introduces the Change Model, you can invite your team members to use it as a reference as you work together on your change initiative.

• **Option Four:** Use FranklinCovey's individual and leader training using the Change Model. Visit FranklinCovey.com to learn more.

How Leaders Create the ROI for Change

By learning how change works and utilizing the Change Model, leaders can reduce the dip in the change curve. They can reduce the duration and impact of the disruption, reap the benefits of the change sooner, and start preparing for the next inevitable waterfall.

As a leader, you can provide clarity in the Zone of Disruption and overcome obstacles in the Zone of Adoption as you give team members permission to try new things. This helps you reduce the time (*x* axis) you and your team spend climbing out (see Figure 14).

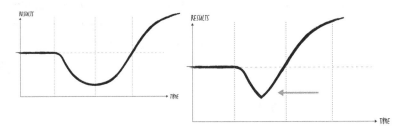

FIGURE 14: *Reducing the Time Spent Climbing Out.*

You can reduce the drop in results (*y* axis) by preparing people for the change in the Zone of Status Quo (see Figure 15). The more they know about an upcoming change and the more they can prepare, the less results will suffer when a change happens.

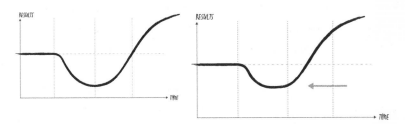

FIGURE 15: *Reducing the Dip in Results.*

Does the dip in results ever go away? No. With change, there is almost always an impact on results. But as an effective leader, you can help your teams reduce the duration and the depth of the dip. And when you reduce the duration and depth of the dip, you lower the costs of the change and move more quickly to the outcomes you were looking for.

Change and Being the Captain

In *Who Rocked the Boat?,* the captain guided the crew through the difficulties they faced, helping them shift from lamenting about what was outside their control to focusing on what they could influence and how they could work together. The captain

Leading change is best accomplished by answering the question, **How do I help my team succeed here?**

demonstrated that leading change is best accomplished by answering the question, *How do I help my team succeed here?* versus issuing commands or simply leaving people to figure things out on their own.

Captain's Corner

Orienting Your Team to the Change

Leaders recognize that those involved in change need the opportunity to orient themselves to the new reality. They benefit from the space to consider and process what they believe and feel their part in the change will be.

To help orient yourself or members of your team, ask:

- Which zone are you in with the change? If you or they answer yes to a question, move to the next one. Your first no tells you where you are.
    - Are we in the Zone of Status Quo: Has the change begun?
    - Are we in the Zone of Disruption: Are you clear about what is changing, why, and what the change means for you (impact on work, responsibilities, personal life, etc.)?
    - Are we in the Zone of Adoption: Have you reached the targeted outcomes of the change?
    - Are we in the Zone of Innovation: Are you making the most of the change? Can you see opportunities emerge from the change besides the expected results?

If the change feels overwhelming, ask the members of your team:

- What about this change feels outside your control?
- What can you control?
- What opportunities might the change create?

The Experience and Mindset of Change

Change can elicit both biological and learned responses from those going through it. Because of this, a change leader is doing more than simply implementing "the new" as a series of tasks. Such leaders may mistakenly feel their primary responsibility is to dictate what must be done, by whom, and by when, then hold the team accountable. But change involving humans—especially when unanticipated or unwanted—is considerably more complex. Effective change leaders understand and empathize with the ways their team members are experiencing change and adopt the necessary mindsets to lead them forward. These two areas are so critical, we've given each an entire chapter (Chapter Three, "How We Experience Change," and Chapter Four, "The Mindset to Lead Change"). It's been our experience that leaders often neglect these vital best practices and are tempted to jump directly to the Change Model. But as you'll see in the next two chapters, this preparatory work is essential to effectively leading change.

> *Effective change leaders understand and empathize with the ways their team members are experiencing change and adopt the necessary mindsets to lead them forward.*

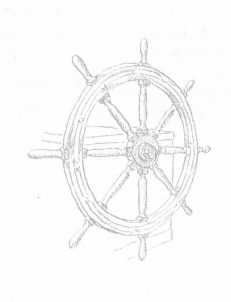

CHAPTER THREE

How We Experience Change

L eaders who fail to account for how their people will experience and react to change are likely doomed before they even start. For example, to the leadership team at a large customer-relationship management (CRM) company, it was an exciting opportunity... a no-brainer, really. They had just announced they were jumping into the non-fungible token (NFT) market, a space that had surged from obscurity to a valuation of over $40 billion at that time.[5] If the company could get a piece of *that* pie (which they felt they could), it would open a valuable new revenue stream.

It was an exciting change, and management was convinced their employees would love it. But when the initiative was announced, hundreds of employees revolted. They protested about the environmental impact of the venture, as well as about the Wild West nature of the NFT market, where scams were prevalent and financial regulation minimal. Employees protested so vehemently, in fact, the company organized listening sessions to better learn about the concerns before moving forward.[6]

Which raises the question: Why were the listening sessions an afterthought rather than part of the early change process? Most likely, because it's easy for leadership to think of change as a process to roll out and manage, instead of considering it a people-centric engagement opportunity.

Often the drivers behind a change feel obvious to the leadership teams and even exciting, logical, and straightforward. Yet, 70 percent of changes fail to reach their intended outcome,[7] so there's a massive disconnect going on. Leaders who initiate change simply see things from a different

It's easy for leadership to think of change as a process to roll out and manage, instead of considering it a people-centric engagement opportunity.

perspective from those tasked with implementing it—a disconnect that can doom a change initiative before it even gets off the ground.

However, you can dramatically increase your odds of success by increasing your understanding of how people experience change, leading them through any emotionally charged reactions, and inviting them to take ownership of what they can control and the new results to strive for.

Our Brains on Change

Consider how we typically feel when change happens: often a mix of apprehension, dread, anxiety, stress, trepidation, and more. Of course, that's not always the case; some change can be serendipitous, pleasantly surprising, and desired. But as humans, we're physically wired to react to change as a threat to our survival. Yet, without change, nothing grows. In a video shown to participants in our *Change* work session, we highlight how the brain works when confronted with change:

> *The brain scans for threat constantly using two parts: the one that acts, and the one that reacts. The thinking brain, the one that acts, can respond consciously, with intention. It plans and prepares. It's where we do our best work. The survival brain reacts unconsciously. This reactive instinct is meant to keep us safe and alive, but it can create havoc if left unchecked.*

> *Here's the bad news: any change, whether large or small, can signal a threat. Once alarmed, both the thinking brain and survival brain fixate on how to manage the threat and return us to safety. And that limits our ability to find good solutions.*

> *Here's the good news: the brain can minimize uncertainty using patterns and routines. For example, once we know the pattern of driving a car, we don't have to think about it; our instincts kick in at the right time and protect us.*

> *As challenging as change can be, there's a predictable pattern to it—one that can help the survival brain cope. When we know how to navigate this pattern, we can engage the thinking brain. And that's how we turn uncertainty into opportunity to make the most of change.*

Despite our biological programming, we yearn for the progress and results that change can bring, whether personally or in our organizations, communities, cultures, societies, and even the world. Knowing that we all see change from different points of view (or experiences, or paradigms) can help us navigate and turn our inherent uncertainty into greater opportunities. Navigating change is more than a leadership or professional competency—it's a *life* competency.

Change Is a Biological and Learned Response

Let's get more nuanced as we expand our definition of "fear" to include everything from "doubt" to "unease" to "concern" to "worry" to "downright debilitating dread." Fear in the face of change can manifest in many ways and usually causes us to slow things down, push back, or find an alternative.

Human beings are born with only two innate fears: the fear of falling and the fear of loud noises.[8] That means other fears are learned. Take Charlie Brown, a youth who stoically deals with life's unwanted changes in the comic strip *Peanuts*, drawn and authored by Charles Schulz. At the time of Schulz's death in 2000, *Peanuts* was running in more than 2,500 newspapers in 75 countries and boasted a readership of over 350 million people. One recurring story involved Charlie's friend Lucy, who would regularly offer to hold a football (American football) so Charlie could take a run at it and then kick it. But each time, as Charlie approached, she pulled the football away at the last moment, causing him to miss and fall flat on his back. The following year (this was a yearly ritual), Lucy would profess to have changed, so Charlie could trust that *this* time things would work out. But Lucy invariably pulled the ball back at the last moment, and Charlie found himself on his back once again. Year after year.

There's likely a change you've wrestled with that feels similar—as if the "ball" has been pulled away at the last moment and you end up flat on your back. We've all been hurt by change, disappointed by change, and perhaps even embarrassed by change. We've had setbacks in our careers, our goals, and our relationships because of change. Our biology and our experiences have reinforced that change can be a huge risk. No wonder, when announcing a change, your team may feel like Charlie Brown and even see you as

Lucy, ready to yank the ball out from under them! The truth is, no matter how emphatically you announce that the change football is there to kick and score with, your team may be holding onto some very justifiable doubts.

In our research leading up the development of our solution and this book, we created an organizational assessment, given to individuals and leaders over the course of nearly a decade, and captured data across numerous industries and government entities (see Figure 16). One question asked was whether a change they were currently facing would make things better or worse for their organization. In response, 72 percent answered "worse" and only 28 percent looked at change as a positive.

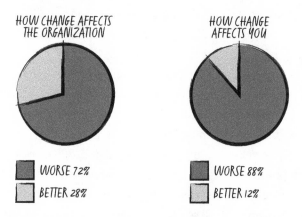

FIGURE 16: How Change Affects You and Your Organization.

Other research confirms our findings—not only do more than two-thirds of change implementations fail to reach their intended outcome,[9] but much of it has to do with how the organization shapes attitudes toward the change.[10] Simply put, a fear of change is unlikely to produce positive outcomes for the individual or the organization.[11] For the leader, understanding the reality of such fear and resistance is the first step in doing something about it. And through the understanding and acknowledgment of those fears, you can build deeper trust.

Andy Cindrich

The Power of Labeling Emotions

I once shared the platform with a client who admitted she was feeling anxious and fearful about our upcoming presentation. As we talked, I explained to her that our brains interpret the physiological state of fear the same way they interpret excitement. To put the anxiety in its place, we merely need to tell our brains that what we are feeling is excitement, rather than allowing our brains to process the feelings as fear.

Best-selling author and professor Brené Brown said it like this: "It's a huge part of the mythology around emotion that if we look it in the eye, it gives it power...the reality is, if we look it in the eye and name it, it gives us power."[12] Simply renaming fear as excitement can keep our lizard brains in check while our problem-solving frontal lobes take control. Some of the chemicals most involved in a "fight, run, or freeze" response are also part of positive emotional states like excitement, happiness, and joy. When our thinking brain tells our emotional brain that we're in a good place, the brain can quickly shift the way we experience the emotion—in this case, from fear to excitement.

When we finished our session, the client I was presenting with shared that the simple advice I'd offered had been game-changing for her (as it was for me when I'd first learned it). And while it's true we don't often control the change that's coming at us, we *can* control how we label the emotions we experience when going through change and turn those feelings into "facts" that work for our benefit.

Change Success Increases When Leaders Provide the Vital Linkage

Change can come from a variety of places: updated regulations, laws, market shifts, customers, research, innovations, shifts in strategic direction, new leadership, mergers and acquisitions, or anything else designed to achieve better results within an organization. Sometimes these inputs are external and other times they are internal (as in a leader deciding on a self-initiated change of some sort).

Regardless of the sources of change, one of the foundational principles we've experienced time and time again through change work is that the success lies in the people. Thus, the role of the leader is to provide the linkage between the source of the change and the people who make it happen.

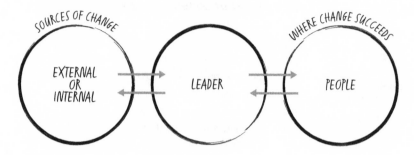

FIGURE 17: *Leaders Provide the Link.*

Notice that the arrows in the above graphic point in both directions. Many leaders tasked with implementing the change often see only the top arrow moving from left to right: a change is initiated, the leader broadcasts what's expected, and their people get to work. Effective leaders implement a more dynamic and fluid approach to change as they:

- Recognize that leaders, formal and not, are all responsible for initiating change.
- See both the strategic and tactical views, providing the essential connection between the two.
- Provide important feedback to senior leaders, acknowledging that the day-to-day realities of a change implementation will push on assumptions, create shortfalls in execution, and force senior leaders to rethink their approach more than once.
- Understand that trying to execute *tactically* against a flawed strategy is doomed to failure.
- Earn their team members' trust by being "in it" with them and not just parroting the words of the change sponsor(s).
- Create safety for trial-and-error failures, turning setbacks into learning opportunities.
- Adjust in real time to the change environment, building collaboration, inviting shared ownership and accountability, and inspiring high levels of engagement throughout.
- Never forget that organizations change *only* when their people do.

Captain's Corner

Find and Communicate the Vital Linkage of Change

Find and share the vital linkage between you, your team, and the organization by asking and answering the following:

Three questions everyone must be able to answer:

- What's changing?
- Why the change?
- What does it mean to me as an individual?

Now, if helpful, expand on the first three questions by asking:

- How does the change link to the organization's strategy? to your team's direction or current initiatives?
- Who wants the change?
- What short- and long-term benefits do you or the organization expect from making this change?
- How might the change affect the tactics, tasks, or processes your team uses to get work done? What challenges does the change present?
- What are the costs of change failure (e.g., decreased trust, a drop in revenue, lower engagement, poor client satisfaction, loss of market share, turnover, increased stress, health issues)?
- As a leader, do I support the change? If not, can I articulate my concerns with my leader and still set aside any lingering disagreements to align with the organizational change?

When communicating to your leaders about obstacles your team is facing, ask yourself:

- What is the nature of the obstacle standing in the way of successfully implementing the change?
- What blind spots might my leaders have regarding these obstacles?
- What can I do to help my leaders better see and understand these obstacles?
- How much tactical information is too much? What might waste my leaders' time or invite micromanagement?

When sharing your leaders' perspectives about the obstacles your team is facing, ask yourself:

- What pushback can I anticipate from my team against the recommendations from upper management and/or the executive sponsors of the change?
- Are there blind spots my team has that I could fill in to help clear things up?
- Am I prepared to communicate the alignment between the organizational values and the strategy for the change to the people with the tactical responsibility to implement it?
- Am I ready and willing to refocus the team on the things they can control versus what they can't?

Change Creates Friction

If a match and a striking surface were both to move simultaneously in the same direction—same speed, same distance—nothing would happen. But if the match head moves quickly in one direction and the striking surface remains fixed, resistance is created, which in turn creates friction and produces fire.

You and your team may feel at odds with a change, in effect moving one way while the change (proverbially rubbing you the wrong way) moves the other. Like a match, you're primed to get "hot" as a result, and perhaps even ignite. This can sound like:

"This change is so stupid! Why are we even doing this?"

"What's wrong with the way it was before?"

"This is *not* what I signed up for!"

Inside every match head is a mix of chemicals, including antimony trisulfide, potassium chlorate, and more. It turns out people aren't so different, with our own mix of chemicals, including cortisol, glutamate, dopamine, oxytocin, and serotonin. Like a match head, these emotional chemicals are ready to ignite, given the right kind of friction—which is exactly what unwanted and unanticipated change brings.

For example, imagine you're making a significant change to a product your company offers. To make that change on schedule, your Product Development team will need to spend several weekends in the office. Since it's universally accepted that most people would rather spend their weekends at home instead of the office, this is going to create friction. So, what can you do as a leader to reduce the friction and potential for flare-ups? Consider these four steps:

- Remember, change is about people. Consider the impact to those you lead: missing their kids' soccer games, putting off plans with friends, having to arrange childcare, increased commuting costs, etc. Having genuine empathy for your team will help you more authentically communicate and lead through the change.
- Make the case for change. Paint a picture of what's compelling enough about the change to make the short-term disruption worth it.
- Be as efficient as possible with the extra work to minimize the time needed. Help everyone understand exactly what they're being asked to do, and make sure they have the required tools and resources at their disposal. Be as organized as possible up front so that the investment of extra time yields the highest possible results.
- Model the behavior you want to see in those you lead. This might mean rolling up your sleeves and joining your team over the weekend (even if it's not absolutely necessary). Showing commitment to both your team and the change can be a leadership win-win.

It would be naïve to suggest that you can always eliminate the friction an unexpected or unwanted change can bring. But if you can slow it down and/or remove some of the resistance, you can keep the rub from igniting into something more.

Captain's Corner

Reducing Friction Through Building Connection

FranklinCovey's *Unconscious Bias* training shares a mechanism for creating connections with others. Because of the inherent friction that comes with unwanted or unanticipated change, using this approach can be helpful for strengthening connections with team members and other stakeholders. Consider the following statements as you reflect on your team and the nature of the change you're experiencing:

- If you don't have empathy or curiosity, you don't make any connection—you don't learn about the other person and can't relate to their situation. You disengage.

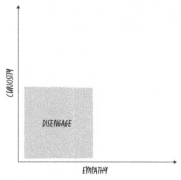

FIGURE 18: *Low Curiosity; Low Empathy.*

- If you have no empathy and high curiosity, you might be making an intellectual connection, but fail to relate to the humanity of the person you're talking to. If you're on the receiving end of the questions, it can feel like you're being interrogated, if not done with care.

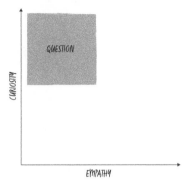

FIGURE 19: *High Curiosity; Low Empathy.*

- If you're high on empathy and don't have any curiosity, you fall into the bottom-right category of "Listen." So you can relate to people on an emotional level, but you may fail to have any rational understanding of the situation. You sympathize, but don't really learn about them or yourself.

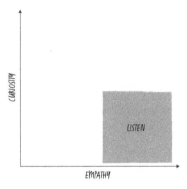

FIGURE 20: *Low Curiosity; High Empathy.*

- When you have high empathy and curiosity, you connect. You see past your biases and preferences and are open to other ways of seeing the world and other options or ideas. Empathy and curiosity fuel each other to create connection.

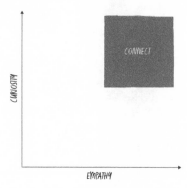

FIGURE 21: *High Curiosity; High Empathy.*

High empathy on its own is too much about the other person; high curiosity on its own is too much about you and your need for information. When you combine high empathy with high curiosity, you can make meaningful connections.

As a change leader, do the following:

1. List the members of your team you feel you have a genuine connection with.
2. List any members of your team you might be lacking empathy for.
   - During your next 1-on-1, ask open-ended questions and be intentional about listening to them. Keep to the 80/20 rule (listening 80 percent of the time and talking only 20 percent). Carry your intentional listening into your other interactions to help build a stronger connection.
3. List any member of your team for whom you might be lacking curiosity.
   - During your next 1-on-1, ask open-ended questions and be genuinely curious to explore the conversation wherever it appropriately takes you. Depending on your levels of trust, it may take some time for the other person to open up. Don't badger them with questions but strike a balance that feels appropriate and remain curious.
4. If you've disengaged with someone, you will likely need to spend time in your intentional expressions of both curiosity and empathy to rebuild the relationship. This might be difficult to do, but if left unresolved, a lack of genuine connection and the trust that ensues can undermine your change efforts. Change, after all, is always about people first.

Marché Pleshette

Learning a Leadership Lesson by Overcoming My Own Change Friction

It's human nature to resist change, and that resistance can become insurmountable in a group setting. Luckily, when others are experiencing resistance to change, leaders can help individuals (and everyone together) make sure to smooth things out for a more pleasant ride.

I experienced change resistance myself a few years ago, when our company updated our employee-reimbursement system. I automatically pushed back on the change. I'd just begun submitting my expenses with relative ease and timeliness through the original system, so I had zero interest in moving to something new. I was experiencing a ton of friction. As it turned out, the new platform required additional steps and processes that felt awkward and used terminology I was unfamiliar with. Whenever my paths crossed with colleagues, there was casual dialogue about the new system. Some commiserated with me, while others suggested they found it to be much easier than expected.

A month passed without my having submitted a single expense report. My psychological resistance to the new system prevented me from leveraging any of the helpful tools and instructions sent out by the organization. It felt inconvenient to even open such support tools. Soon I was getting notes about my lagging willingness to start using the new system (not to mention the company debt I was carrying on my personal credit card!). At first, they were friendly reminders to submit my reports. Then I began to receive more firm nudges, informing me I was holding up the revenue flow, as invoices could not be sent to clients until all related expenses were submitted. Yes, I was a broken link in an organization-wide system because of my resistance to change!

You'd think that thousands of dollars of accumulated reimbursements would have been worth my effort to change, as I was clearly withholding monies from myself! But even with *that*, I was struggling to overcome my internal resistance to the change.

I finally accepted the reality that this new system was going to be *the* system. It wasn't changing, so I would have to. And that required growth beyond just becoming familiar with the new expense process—it required growth around my perspective regarding change, period. The realization that I was the source of the friction I was experiencing caused me to take a deeper look at what was going on inside. I knew I was a better professional, held a more teachable intellect, and strived to be a more responsible individual than what I was demonstrating. I accepted the fact that I was holding a pessimistic view about the new process, that I had not bothered to understand or empathize with those who championed the change, and that I'd put off dealing with the challenges of learning a new platform because of my preference for the familiar. In that realization, I also had a choice to reject those points of resistance and thus reduce the friction of what I was experiencing.

I chose to change my thinking.

I painstakingly got into the portal and worked through at least ten expenses at one go. It seemed like it took forever, and it was more challenging than it should have been because of my own pileup. This is also where help from leadership came into play. Understanding the *why* behind the *what* helped the whole transition make sense to me. The managing director shared how the system technologically enabled more entities to connect on the back end, further facilitating a more expedient process for bringing in revenue. She could see the challenge the change had presented to many other team members, and her words were reassuring: "I promise it will get easier and faster as we get more proficient. I know it has been a bit frustrating at the beginning, but we are heading into the twenty-first century with some *great* technology!"

By the way, I mastered the employee-reimbursement system not long after that. In fact, I started to see for myself the benefits the new system offered that were much better than the previous one. I would never have known that without overcoming my resistance. Fortunately, my transition during change happens a lot more expediently today because I've learned to see the value in change, the necessity of change, and the infinite reality that change will happen. What is important to note, however, is that I did not journey through the change process alone or ashamed. There was dialogue, respect, understanding, and resources always present.

When leaders consider that change is a deeply human experience and allow themselves to relate, their capacity to support their team members through the process is unleashed. If leaders are ever to accomplish set goals, we must make it a priority to navigate the process of change and do it with compassion. Leaders are the impetus of change and outcomes, but people make it happen. Remember what it was like before you conquered the uncertainty of change, then honor your team with support to get beyond the friction.

Change Comes in Waves

Change is never a "one and done" event. Every pursuit in life is about change on some level, either as the goal itself or a byproduct from trying to achieve it. But that doesn't mean there isn't a rhythm to change, especially when change is unexpected and driven by outside forces. Effective change leaders take advantage of change rhythms and are conscientious about what happens "between" the waves.

Andy Cindrich

Surfing and Change

As the sun was setting at a popular surf spot near Kailua-Kona, Hawaii, I noticed two young surfers on the shore's lava-rock platform. They leaped onto their boards and into the surf, paddling gracefully and eagerly toward the approaching whitewater soup. Four- to five-foot-high waves broke in the distance. As the waves approached, the youngsters, cheered on by some teenagers and adults standing on the seawall, duck-dived their boards beneath the turbulent mix of foam, force, and sand to pop up on the other side of the passing wave and continue their efforts to get past what's called the impact zone.

I watched these two young surfers repeat this process for the next fifteen minutes without ever being able to make it out to where the older surfers were calmly sitting on their boards. Seeing that the youngsters lacked the strength and stamina to battle the pounding surf much longer, an adult called the boys back to shore.

It struck me, as I watched this scene play out, that there was a leadership lesson at work for how people respond to change. Sometimes you'll have Movers who excitedly jump into the change waters, only to find that they don't have the capability to get to where they intended. They can fight the change forces and pounding surf only so many times before they get frustrated or discouraged. Having never learned to duck-dive properly, the boys in Hawaii were doomed to get pummeled by each successive wave. And yet, they no doubt learned a great deal about the ocean as a result. They came out of the water tired but stronger and more knowledgeable about what it was going to take for them to surf that break in the future.

Leaders may be hesitant to allow the inexperienced and overconfident into their change surf, but I think that's a mistake. The two young surfers were under adult supervision, which included highly trained lifeguards—protections were in place. Leaders can play a lifeguard-like role as well, drawing on their expertise to monitor the situation and those in it. Further, it's important for leaders to let their people struggle with the challenges of change for a bit and not be too quick to jump in for the rescue. As American author Simon Sinek says, "Innovation is born from the struggle."[13]

Leaders should not only be on the watch for how their people respond to (and struggle with) change but also be willing to get into the water with them and help them understand what's happening and why. The best change leaders provide a safe space for their team to work against the riptides, waves, and whitewater while simultaneously protecting them from exhaustion, frustration, and the danger of the unknown. It's a balancing act, to be sure, and one aligned with the get-ready idiom "Surf's up!"

Captain's Corner

Teaching Your Team to Surf the Change Waves

As a leader, being in the water with your "surfers" too long or too early can hinder successful change. And simply yelling instructions from the shoreline can feel like you're micromanaging your team and diminish, rather than enable, their success. Consider your current or upcoming change and answer the following:

- Does my team know how to "surf" on their own?
- Who are my strong "change" surfers?
  - Am I cheering them on or yelling directions at them from the shore?
- Who are my newbies just trying to paddle out past the break?
  - Have I taught them the fundamentals, or am I constantly jumping in to keep them from "going under"?

Change Means You're Not Always the Captain

Sometimes leading change isn't about holding a formal captain's position or even having your hand on the helm. As a leader, you'll likely get invited into the change initiatives of others, professional and personal. In other words, you'll be asked to step onto another's boat.

Getting in Another's Boat

One twist about the people-centric nature of change is that we're often impacted by others experiencing and going through it. Change is multifaceted and multilayered. It involves growth and growing pains; receiving and breaking unexpected news; and the deep processing of thoughts and feelings. By its very nature, it often evokes fear and uncertainty, and almost always creates a visceral

Marché Pleshette

shift from how we've grown accustomed to experiencing people and circumstances to the acceptance of the new edition of all that has changed. We're not limited to only responding to change, but we're often nudged by an inner voice that compels us to proactively be the change—the difference—in current conditions and possibilities of better things and better days, personally, professionally, domestically, and in world affairs. Whatever the change, the question becomes, "How do I navigate the impact of other people's changes?"

In *Who Rocked the Boat?*, the captain warns the crew that change is coming. When dealing with the unexpected change of others, it can feel oddly like there is no captain and we've been onboarded right at the waterfall's edge.

So how do we react when a change external to us pulls us into the boat—one we didn't ask to board, but suddenly find ourselves in for the ride? We are, after all, more concerned with those in the boat than how seaworthy the vessel happens to be.

Might I suggest we begin with an extra dose of empathy? As we free ourselves of inner resistance, we can take ownership of our role in the change—not so much the change itself, but our role in supporting those going through it. Once you find yourself in another's boat, take stock of what helpful role you can play by staying in the boat, instead of jumping into the water and swimming hard for the shore.

Change is the one constant in life. Of all things good and bad, it's the one thing we can count on to always show up. Said the caterpillar to the butterfly while contemplating this topic, "You've changed."

To which the butterfly replied, "Yes... we're supposed to."

And so too for us... and all the newly emerged "butterflies" circling our heads.

Captain's Corner

The Human Side of Change

Consider the potential costs of change. In FranklinCovey's *The 6 Critical Practices for Leading a Team*, we teach that during stressful times like going through change, your team members are:

- Two and a half times as likely to report prolonged stress.
- Four times as likely to have physical ailments.
- Three times as likely to look for a new job.

Given the above, consider your own experience with a change initiative that didn't go as expected:

- What were the costs to you, your team, and your organization?
- What leader behaviors might have inadvertently contributed to the cost?
- Did you experience any of the above (stress, physical ailments, looking for a new job)?

What have you learned from your own experience around change that can help you better lead others through it?

Moving from Understanding Change to Adopting a Leadership Mindset

Now that you've invested the time and energy to better understand how your team is experiencing change, you'll want to turn inward and adopt the mindset to lead the change successfully. Being intentional about this skill is vital because the tactics for moving through each zone will differ, but the undergirding mindset will stay fixed, providing the necessary foundation for your team's success. As we mentioned previously, it's tempting for leaders to undervalue this preparatory work and jump directly into the Change Model. It's been our experience that leaders who succeed at change are focused on their people first, while holding an intentional mindset through it—a mindset we'll explore more deeply in the next chapter.

CHAPTER FOUR

The Mindset to Lead Change

U RGENT. IMPORTANT. NOW. FASTER. DELIVER.

Leaders today are busier than ever. They generally are stretched thin on resources and time, while organizations want new changes implemented as quickly as possible. It is not surprising that, as a change is launched, leaders want to get things moving—now. They jump right into the middle of the Change Model, moving at top speed to get it done.

Urgency and speed are not the perfect recipe for change success. Why? Because change is a people business. At the start of a change with people, fast is slow and slow is fast.

Your success leading a team through change will be greatly improved if you give consideration to a few foundational mindset needs that exist for you and your people.

Help Move People From Chaos and Uncertainty to Order and Predictability

If a leader's mindset about change is chaotic and uncertain, the odds of success are greatly diminished. The Change Model framework provides an ordered and predictable way for leaders to think about and lead through change. Leaning into the language of the *Who Rocked the Boat?* parable, the framework functions like a *compass* to determine where we are and a *map* to chart what lies ahead.

The Change Model framework further orients leaders to their responsibility within each zone:

The Change Model framework functions as a compass to determine where you are and a map to chart what lies ahead.

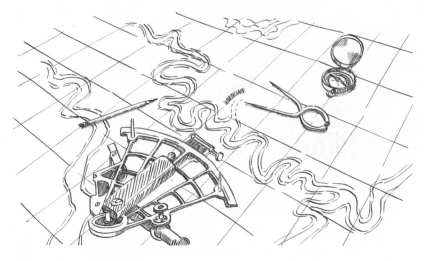

Figure 22: *Map and Compass.*

- **Zone of Status Quo:** *preparing* your team for change.
- **Zone of Disruption:** *clarifying* the what, why, and impact of the change.
- **Zone of Adoption:** inspiring your team to *persist* through the change.
- **Zone of Innovation:** inviting your team to *explore* new possibilities because of the change.

Leaders Need a Framework to Think About and Manage Change

Curtis Bateman

An executive at one of our major clients shared his experience using the Change Model as a framework to lead change: "This has been the best help on change, and it addressed things we could not have even foreseen. It's gone better than any change I've previously implemented at my current company and all the years at my previous company."

For such a big impact, you'd think, as consultants, that we had spent an enormous amount of time with this company, helping them overhaul their systems and recommending changes to achieve these significant results. But what we gave them was simple. In a short amount of time, I interviewed five executives and then taught them the four zones in the Change Model. It was remarkable to see how quickly each of them identified which zone they were in. Further, this awareness led them to understand that some of them were further ahead than others on their team, and that the same was likely happening throughout the rest of the organization. This "map" and "compass" perspective led to the necessary mindset to make sense of the change and lead the organization forward.

Winning at the Change Game

The year was 1891, and James Naismith had a challenge on his hands: he was to lead a physical education class for a bunch of restless and unruly college students with a lot of energy to burn off. The students had just finished their American football season and had a long winter ahead of them before spring sports began. Other teachers had tried to manage their pent-up need for physical activity—all had failed. With blizzards raging outside, the students were roughhousing in the halls and in the gymnasium, causing a persistent problem for the Massachusetts school.

Thirty-one-year-old Naismith had only recently joined the teaching staff at the International YMCA Training School (later Springfield College) when the school leaders tasked him with establishing some order in the gym. He was to organize the young men into activity groups, directing their energy in ways that would keep them engaged and fit.

As Naismith studied out the problem to devise a plan, he realized, "The trouble is not with the men, but with the system that we are using."[14] He needed a better framework.

He wondered what kind of game would work indoors and be fun to play. He considered rugby, American football, lacrosse, and soccer, pondering the rules and equipment, and the constraints of being indoors. And then an idea hit him. He nailed two peach baskets to opposite walls, handed the young men a soccer ball, and told them to try to throw the ball into the opposing team's basket. The game of basketball was born.

But the first game looked more like a mix of football and boxing, with players tackling each other and even throwing blows. When the first match was over (or perhaps better said "was broken up"), one boy had been knocked unconscious, another had a dislocated shoulder, and many of them had black eyes and cut lips.[15]

The game needed structure. Naismith went back to the drawing board and came up with thirteen rules that established order—a framework. He channeled the students' energies in ways that were not only easily understood but also engaging, motivating, and inspiring. Soon the game became a hit. Basketball grew in popularity among students at other local schools, then around the country, and eventually the world.

Much like Naismith's framework for basketball, the Change Model can channel the pent-up energy of your team in ways that are easily understood, engaging, and with the right vision and inspiration, even fun.

Developing a Common Language for Change

When it comes to change, it can feel like leadership is speaking one language and the rest of the organization another. A statement like "We're changing to increase efficiency" can be easily heard as "The company is trying to automate my job so they can fire me." Using the framework as a guide, a leader would be more intentional about not only communicating the *why*, but filling in the *what* and the *impact*. This counters the predisposition to see change as a threat, which leads to team members filling in the blanks themselves, likely with a dour outlook (more on this in Chapter Six: "The Zone of Disruption"). Or consider the difference between announcing, "I know it's chaotic right now, but we'll eventually weather the storm," and saying, "We're in the Zone of Disruption, so we have an important decision to make to move us forward."

The Change Model and the reactions to change give you a common language that can get you onto the same page. Imagine asking a team member, "Which Zone do you believe we're in?" They might say, "Oh, we're in the Zone of Adoption, for sure." And then another would add, "No, we're not. We haven't even reached the Point of Decision yet." How much more productive are these kinds of conversations than your team wallowing in a victim mentality or hyperfocused on the disruption and ensuing emotions?

Make It Safe to Discuss Change

We've seen plenty of change discussions devolve into defensiveness and blame. As a leader, you may have to keep steering people back to the Change Model framework if you find this to be the case. What a difference it makes pointing to the model and announcing, "I feel like *Move* at the base of the cliff right now," rather than saying, "I'm tired of waiting around for others to get this done—nobody seems to want to change around here but me." When your team is pointing at the framework, they're *not* pointing at each other.

Your goal as a leader is to help your people step outside of themselves and identify the reaction to change without feeling they *are* that reaction.

> **When your team is pointing at the framework, they're not pointing at each other.**

 ## Captain's Corner

Use the Language of Change for Less Threatening Discussions

The Change Model and the Five Common Reactions to Change give teams the language and framework to talk about change. Effective change leaders foster open discussions about the change they and their teams are going through, reducing resistance and defensiveness.

1. With your team, draw the Change Model and list the Change Reactions on a whiteboard.

2. Lead a discussion by asking:
   - Where do you think we are in our current change? (Have multiple people indicate where they think they are on the Change Model.)
   - What reaction best represents you now? (You might keep a tally: "Okay, so I'm seeing three Waits, two Resists, and one Minimize.")
   - What are we thinking, feeling, and doing because of being in this zone?

     Note: As a leader, it can take a bit of finesse as you lead this discussion, and sometimes there is overlap, as feelings in the Zone of Disruption can be similar or identical to feelings in the Zone of Adoption, etc. Our experience is that teams mostly get it right, but it's not essential that they're 100 percent dialed in to the specific language of each zone. It may feel awkward at first, as you get your people in the room and lead this discussion, but you'll get better at it with practice. And take solace in the fact that simply asking how your team is thinking, feeling, and doing goes a long way to engender the safe and open dialogue critical to change success.

Christi Phillips

Using the Language of Change (EMR Adoption, Part One)

You may recall from my introduction that I was involved in a large healthcare change initiative early in my career. As the four authors met to discuss the various points of view we could share in our "author asides" throughout this book, we decided a running story might prove useful. After all, what was going on in the healthcare industry was a *massive* change that continues to this day. Given the number of people involved, the integration of new technology, the breaking of long-entrenched habits, challenging organizational hierarchies, and ultimately being responsible for highly sensitive and private medical data, both the complexities and the stakes were high. As such, I'll carry this story through several of my author asides as we examine how aspects of such a monumental and systemic change showed up in different ways and various places along the change journey.

The organization I worked for was comprised of many medical facilities and freestanding hospitals needing to transition to electronic medical record (EMR) systems. My role was to coach healthcare leaders and help them acknowledge up front that the people they were trying to lead weren't particularly interested in changing. That's the same for most people. The leaders may see the need for the change and may be excited about a change, but that doesn't necessarily mean their people are. People are in their status quo for a reason, and to be shaken out of that known and comfortable space, their River Routine, is not something most people would ask for. In almost every instance, people need to be talked through the change. In fact, as a leader of change, that's your primary role—to talk your people through.

I remember hearing about a guy who was in a small airplane when the pilot passed out. The man had no flight experience, but he gained control of the plane and now had to figure out how to land it. His status quo had been a normal flight with an experienced pilot at the controls. This change was not something he would have asked for! But he did have a resource to help him. He radioed air traffic controllers and told them about his situation. They put someone on the radio who had many years of experience as a flight instructor. This flight instructor carefully talked him through and coached him and helped him land the plane safely. As we rolled out our EMR system, our nurses felt encumbered. They felt the weight of the change. And even though our IT people would take care of the systems, to our nurses it felt difficult and confusing, maybe like flying a plane with no experience.

In leading change, I've learned that leaders become like that flight instructor. People are dealing with changes that may seem almost as scary to them as realizing their pilot has passed out in the seat next to them. Leaders need to learn to talk people through the change. Help them land the plane. A leader can't just say, "We're making a change," and expect success without ongoing communication and guidance. Imagine if the flight instructor had said, "The nearest airport is thirty miles southeast of your current location. Good luck!" and closed off communication. Leading change takes an extraordinary level of patience, guidance, listening, coaching, and discussion throughout. You can't just describe the *destination*, you also have to get people involved in the route to get there. Which takes us to my next lesson about communication.

Good communication requires a common language. That's what we've provided with the Change Model and the Five Common Reactions to Change. They are that common language that enables a shared culture, and that's crucial when leading any team through change. As that flight instructor coached the passenger flying the plane, who likely didn't know the names or functions of the controls, the instructor probably had to be very explicit with information and say things like, "That gauge to the left, that's the altimeter. Here's what that's for..." They could build up a vocabulary that allowed them to communicate and possibly even alleviate some confusion for the fledgling "pilot." You can do the same with the language of change. After you've described the destination to your people, your common language can be a kind of verbal shorthand along the way, like, "Right now, we're in the Zone of Disruption," and you and your people will all know what that means. Someone you lead could say something like, "I'm feeling like *Resist*, or *Move*, or *Wait*, right now," and you'd both know what that means as well, and you'd be able to talk about it. You'd have that common language. In fact, this is one of the remarkable outcomes of Dr. Covey's bestselling book *The 7 Habits of Highly Effective People*. Since its publication over thirty years ago, literally tens of millions of people have either read the book or attended FranklinCovey's work session, enabling them to both talk about and work through issues that they might have historically been referring to using different and even conflicting terms. It's an invaluable resource for creating common ground and speeding up the pace and clarity of communication in cultures in which you have competent people of wildly differing educations, backgrounds, and even expertise.

My third and final lesson from this experience is that the language of change isn't just for leaders. It works best when used by all team members to communicate with each other, and to move a change forward. As the system implementation rolled along, I had some nurses and staff who were good at championing the change and speaking positively of the change, while others continued to be challenged by the ongoing, uphill effort. In their regular huddles, nurses and their leaders would talk through their feelings as this new thing became an integrated part of their work environment. Kudos to their initiative and instincts. Their feedback—positive and negative—when shared with the implementation teams made the outcome even better, because it pointed out things that project managers and leaders simply had not considered.

Like the pilot and the flight instructor, we eventually landed the EMR, but only after several failed attempts at the runway. A few team members chose to exit the company because working through the change just seemed too hard. Imagine if we had had the shared benefit of the common vernacular of the Change Model available to the entire project team. It would have allowed us to surface everyone's reactions, questions, concerns, and successes even more effectively. If we had known some were feeling like *Quit* and *Quits*, we might have done a better job of making it safe to talk about what was needed to keep them on board.

Messaging a Change Vision

Many leaders make a change announcement and then move on to other things, expecting the change to just happen. After such pronouncements, if people are less than enthusiastic, are dragging their feet, or are downright hostile, leaders respond with phrases like "Embrace change," or "Change or die." That's about as helpful as telling a seven-year-old to "Embrace broccoli." Simply saying "Embrace change" sends the message that people just need to get on board, no questions asked. That may create compliance for a time, but generally fails to create a culture of change where people choose a high level of ownership, alignment, and engagement. As a reminder, leaders don't create engagement. You can't force someone to be engaged. What leaders can do, especially amid change, is to create a culture where people choose to offer their highest level of contribution (which is paramount during any change initiative).

There are several needs your team members have when it comes to change. For example, your team needs:

- To know why they're doing something.
- To be brought into a vision of what's ahead.
- To determine whether a change is worth it.
- To believe that they, and those around them, can put in the necessary effort and pull it off—that your strategy for change will work.
- To opt in and decide to go on the change journey with you.
- To trust you and others on the team.
- To know the truth. (Unfortunately, many change leaders either assume that difficult truths have filtered down to their team members or feel they are doing their teams a service by shielding them from difficult things.)

We'll take a deeper look at creating a vision of the change in Chapter Five: "The Zone of Status Quo."

Communicate More Than a Change Announcement

In the early 1960s, France's Minister of Cultural Affairs, André Malraux, commissioned artist Marc Chagall to paint the ceiling of the Paris Opera, the Palais Garnier. The proposed change caused a storm of controversy, as Parisians were upset about the commission on several levels: *Why paint over the original artwork? Why use a modern art style for a historic building? Why choose a Lithuanian-born Jewish painter to do the work?* But Malraux didn't just make the change announcement and leave Chagall to face the protesters alone and figure it out. Instead, the Minister of Cultural Affairs stayed engaged, listening to his critics, and offering a different narrative. In the end, Malraux effectively countered those stirring the pot of controversy so that Chagall and his team could work and make the desired change happen.

FIGURE 23: *The Palais Garnier.*

The paintings eventually won over many of the early doubters and became a benchmark for how to integrate modernism into France's historic landmarks. Today Chagall's ceiling is one of the Opera's most popular attractions. The lesson here is that it can be tempting for leaders to equate change *communication* with making a change *announcement*. But change success requires ongoing dialogue and involvement from those leading it.

> *Change success requires ongoing dialogue and involvement from those leading it.*

Such open and ongoing communication doesn't seem to be the norm, however. In a 2017 study of over 27,000 employees, 65 percent didn't think their organizations shared enough about the challenges they were facing.[16]

So tell it straight. People deserve to know. But also, recognize there's power in what you choose to name the things associated with your change.

Sometimes It's All in the Name

Andy Cindrich

I once worked with a company in the U.S. Pacific Northwest where the compliance department was at war with almost every other department in the company. Sales referred to this team as the "sales prevention unit" of the company! Manufacturing was frustrated with all the Compliance rules, and R&D disliked the unending hoops they had to jump through to get anything approved. We decided to work on the department's internal branding as part of the change effort. What everyone in the company wanted was the ability to introduce their devices into the huge markets of what were historically known as the BRIC nations (Brazil, Russia, India, and China).

As I worked with the Compliance team, we decided a name change could go a long way toward reframing the other departments' paradigm about the role of compliance. The new name, Market Access, communicated to others the real purpose of the team. The name change signaled a different intent and communicated purpose in a way the other name never could. And sometimes that simplicity is enough. In our story, the resultant paradigm change laid the foundation for the team itself and former adversaries in Sales, Marketing, R&D, and Manufacturing to become collaborative partners. They now sought out the new Market Access team to help solve problems and open doors, rather than constantly trying to keep the Compliance team from finding out what they were up to!

When it comes to change, names matter. Having a shared vocabulary and being intentional about how we label and talk about change can go a long way to head off ineffective and counterproductive behaviors like avoidance, conflict, suspicion, and suboptimization.

Know What's Appropriate to Share (and What's Not)

If there's a pattern we've seen time and time again with change, it's that while leaders shouldn't share everything, they're almost always not sharing enough.

Share what's necessary for people to handle the change and be transparent that there may be information that is not available for distribution. There are cases when it's not only inappropriate but even illegal to share certain things. In addition, sometimes a leader simply doesn't know all the answers about the change. If that's the case, share that you don't know. People respect openness and humility. When you don't know, say you don't know, and tell your team that, together, you'll find the answers. The adage says, "People can handle bad news; they can't handle wrong news or no news." It's worth noting that, as a leader, you've probably had a lot more

> **While leaders shouldn't share everything, they're almost always not sharing enough.**

time to digest and prepare for the change. It's likely that your team is hearing about it from you for the first time. Give them time to understand the *what*, *why*, and personal *impact* of the current change. You're not simply initiating a change by announcing it to your team. Instead, you're committing to an ongoing dialogue that you will need to have throughout the change process.

Inviting Others to Opt In

Search and rescue workers brave extreme conditions to save a life. World-class athletes work incessantly on improving their strength, skills, and stamina. Parents whose child is fighting an illness will go to great lengths to find a solution and provide comfort. As humans, we have the capacity to move heaven and earth if there's a strong enough *why*. So, as a leader, give your people a *why* so they can make the choice to opt in and succeed at change.

The Sound of Change

For several years, I managed an Employee Retention department. During my tenure, I had many conversations with a range of employees and leaders to better understand why, at times, we saw so much turnover and what we could do to make ourselves an employer of choice. I gathered insight and data from stay conversations, exit interviews, and employee-engagement surveys, as well as from general observations of leadership styles and interactions among individual contributors, teams, and customers.

Marché Pleshette

Ninety percent of the time when employees resigned, we'd hear about valid challenges, but challenges made worse by managers' lack of communication or their mandates to team members to just "get with the program." These managers often failed to share the *why* behind very important responsibilities or, in many instances, share the reason change was happening. I clearly saw the autocratic/dictatorial ways of leading (versus collaborative leadership) deprive team members of the benefit of understanding how they played into the big picture and what they could do to be more meaningful contributors.

With over eight thousand employees, change was happening every day—sometimes on departmental levels and sometimes systemwide. But even subtle shifts in day-to-day functions can be disruptive. Smaller changes are still change. A new leader for a team is change! Schedule changes are change. Improvement is change. New strategies and styles of implementing them create change. And the expectation anyone might opt in to change without the opportunity to clearly understand and freely share their insights, feelings, and ideas regarding the change diminishes the likelihood of them ever opting in.

During exit interviews, I heard repeatedly, "My manager was not listening." Essentially, they were expressing that, as frontline employees, they had rich insights and suggestions and they wanted to be heard. Because they felt undervalued as contributors, they opted out rather than opting in. Without dialogue and inclusion of the very people we needed to make change happen, we lost them.

So listen to your people. Will everything they say be pure wisdom? Of course not. Might much of what they say be complaints unaccompanied by possible solutions? Perhaps. Could the things they want be at odds with what the company wants? Maybe. But the common thread that runs through all of these is simply that people want to be heard.

Today we're living in a world where people are opting out—"The Great Resignation," quiet quitting, the refusal to be led by mediocrity. After all, people don't quit jobs; they quit bad leaders and dysfunctional and toxic cultures. To paraphrase John Maxwell, *If you think you're leading and no one is following, you're merely taking a walk.*

Clearing the Path

Some obstacles associated with a change are bigger than what one person or a team can handle. Leaders need to jump in and clear the path. In our previous example of the repainting of the Paris Opera House, Minister of Cultural Affairs André Malraux intervened as a leader to address people's concerns about Chagall painting over the old work: *Why sully a perfectly good piece of artistic history?* In response, Malraux worked with his critics to come up with a solution. Rather than having Chagall paint over the existing ceiling, he asked the artist to paint his work on large cloth panels that would be stretched over the ceiling. That would preserve the original work while displaying Chagall's at the same time.[17] Without Malraux's clearing of roadblocks, Chagall would not have been able to complete his masterpiece.

Clearing the Path Doesn't Mean Solving Everything

While some obstacles need to be cleared by leaders, others should be solved by those doing the work. Sometimes leaders mistakenly believe that "being engaged" means micromanaging—that they need to sign off on every detail and be the source of solutions for everything. They don't. Most problems are best solved by the people closest to the problem. Let your people solve most problems. Don't "snoopervise." Don't become the bottleneck. Don't hover.

> **Most problems are best solved by the people closest to the problem.**

Minister of Cultural Affairs André Malraux was an art theorist, a lover of the arts, and an author. But he wasn't a painter. He left the painting work, and the problems and challenges of the painting, to Chagall. Malraux let Chagall solve the problems of how to create the art on the cloth panels, rather than directly on the ceiling. For the frames to fit under the ceiling, the cloth panels would necessarily be of slightly different dimensions than the ceiling. How much different? What were the dimensions? Not Malraux's problem. That was for Chagall to figure out. How to connect the frames to the ceiling without damaging the previous artwork? That was also best solved by Chagall. What artistic style, colors, and imagery would be a tribute to the Palais Garnier and not an embarrassing eyesore? Again, he left that for Chagall to ponder and come up with a solution.

What Staying Engaged Means for Change Leaders

Engaged change leaders empower their team members to solve problems within their Circle of Influence, rather than getting bogged down in their Circle of Concern:

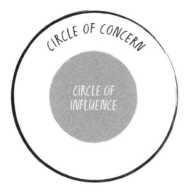

FIGURE 24: *Solve Problems Within Your Circle of Influence.*

As Dr. Stephen R. Covey first wrote about in *The 7 Habits of Highly Effective People*, the Circle of Concern is comprised of the things over which we have no real control. Be Proactive® (Habit 1) means working within our Circle of Influence, or on those things we *can* control. Helping your team become proactive problem solvers will grow their Circle of Influence over time, helping them be better prepared for the next change that will come their way.

An engaged change leader helps their team understand what falls within their Circle of Concern and Circle of Influence. Further, they:

Helping your team become proactive problem solvers will grow their Circle of Influence, helping them be better prepared for the next change that will come their way.

- ◆ **Prepare** their team members for inevitable change, communicate a compelling vision or story of the change, and anticipate obstacles.
- ◆ **Understand** that results will suffer. This is no reason to blame or berate. Rather, it's a time to help people get their sea legs, reorient themselves, and understand what's going on—a time to provide clarity (lots of it), so that people opt in.
- ◆ **Empathize** with their team members, knowing there's a tough slog ahead. They don't sugarcoat it, but they do work to inspire their team members to persist and keep going. This is not the time to sit comfortably

in your office while your team is in the trenches—they need to see you with your sleeves rolled up.

◆ **Stay engaged** throughout to explore and leverage the potential benefits from the change.

Captain's Corner

Clearing the Path or Blocking the Path?

When going through change, your team sometimes needs you to be out in front, clearing the path. At other times, they need you to get out of the way. To better understand whether you're clearing roadblocks, or you are the roadblock, you might ask your team these questions in team meetings or in 1-on-1s:

- As we've been going through this change, how have I been impacting your work?
  - Like a bulldozer, clearing away problems and red tape so you can move forward?
  - Like a mosquito, hovering right by you, micromanaging, and distracting you from your work?
  - Like road construction, causing a bottleneck that's slowing you down?
- Can you share examples about what I'm doing that's slowing you down or making things easier for you?
- To help our team be successful in this change, what would you like to see me do more of or less of? (Note: This requires a high degree of vulnerability in you as a leader. But doing so will build the trust and confidence necessary to lead through the difficulties ahead.)

Moving Through the Change Model

Now that you've progressed through the preparatory work of recognizing how your team experiences change and the mindset you should adopt to lead them forward successfully, it's time to go deeper into the Change Model itself. We'll devote the remaining chapters to each of the four zones, including a chapter on the critical Point of Decision that marks the transition from the bottom of the Disruption "dip" to the climb out of the chasm (and the even higher results that await).

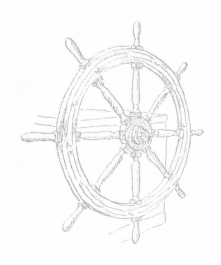

CHAPTER FIVE

The Zone of Status Quo

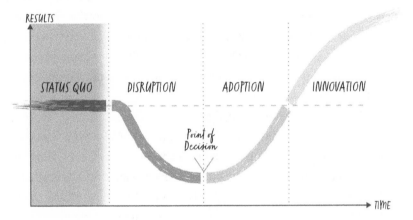

FIGURE 25: *The Zone of Status Quo.*

Preparing for Change

T he Zone of Status Quo is what we experience before a change happens. Here we conduct our "business as usual," even if it's busy and stressful—it's still familiar. In the Zone of Status Quo, leaders prepare their teams for future change as they:

- ◆ **Scan** for trends, patterns, or plans.
- ◆ **Ask** for others' perspectives.
- ◆ **Act** to get better organized.

Reactions in the Zone of Status Quo

Let's return to *Who Rocked the Boat?* to review the crew's reactions in the Zone of Status Quo. At the beginning of the journey, the crew was at ease and settled into their routines. They had work to do and jobs to perform, but it was well within their comfort zone—each knew exactly what was expected of them and how to deliver. So much so, in fact, that when *Move* suggested they use the extra time to sharpen their skills and learn something new, the rest of the crew were dismissive.

Without the tension of a threatening change, it's easy for the Zone of Status Quo to create a false sense of security. It very well could be that the captain—assuming the captain is working for a company—and upper management are all quite pleased with what's going on. The revenue, growth, and margins might all be doing well and even trending in the right direction. But what's tricky about the Zone of Status Quo is that it can feel like you're winning in the moment, with morale high and the future full of promise, yet change is lurking around the bend. Sooner or later, the River Routine erupts into a rapid, followed by a waterfall.

Which is exactly what happened to the ship *Results*.

The first to react in the Zone of Status Quo was *Move*, who "loved the excitement of a new adventure, grabbed a shovel, and began heaping coal into the boilers." Anyone with a natural tendency to move will be excited by the prospect of change. They don't need a lot of information or facts; they're primed and ready to go, often taking off well ahead of the others.

Minimize will want to know what's expected and change as little as possible as a result. As the character asked in the parable, "Is it *really* a waterfall? Let's not be doing any more than we have to."

Wait, as the name implies, is not in a hurry to do anything fast. They'll adapt to change, albeit slowly, and usually after everyone else is on board. "'I've been fooled by such noises before. Best to hold off and see what happens,' *Wait* said..."

Resist actively fought against the change represented by the waterfall. "We must fight against the pull of the current! Help me throw the anchor overboard!" *Resist* will privately or publicly rebuff the change. Here it's worth noting again that none of the reactions are inherently right or wrong. *Resist* may have had exactly the right instincts to avoid a potentially disastrous change. This is why preparation in the Zone of Status Quo is so critical. Being as informed and prepared as possible can buffer emotional, fear-based reactions.

Those who quit, found in the parable as the twins *Quits* and *Quit*, represent the two final change reactions in the Zone of Status Quo: to quit and leave, or to quit and stay (or quiet quitting). *Quits* chose the former: "'Good luck to you, but I'm outta here!' Then *Quits* jumped overboard and swam for shore." One could ask which is worse—quitting and staying, or quitting and leaving—and question how much time a leader should invest in trying to keep someone like *Quits* on board—especially when they hold a key position. That will be an individual decision, but our experience is if those on your crew can't come to find their own degree of ownership in the change, they are always at risk of disengaging—which applies to *Quit,* who "wanted out but wasn't ready to abandon the ship or crew just yet." So *Quit* didn't leave the ship, but refused to engage with the change.

Christi Phillips

Laying the Groundwork for Change (EMR Adoption, Part Two)

Leaders don't get the luxury of claiming to be surprised by change. When change comes in the form of legislation or regulations, it can be tempting to just shrug your shoulders and give in to its inevitability. Effective change leaders, however, ask what they can do about the change *now* and get to work.

Back to our story of EMR adoption. Imagine you're working in a large and busy hospital. Nurses, physicians, aides, and specialists see hundreds, if not thousands, of patients every week. They perform tests, give medications, and draw samples. And they keep all the records for these visits on paper medical charts and computer programs not integrated with the broader system.

This was the state of healthcare globally before the advent of electronic medical records (EMRs) in the 1970s. Introducing EMRs would come to impact all aspects of healthcare delivery. Not only would they help manage ballooning costs, they would also increase patient satisfaction and care quality. EMRs allowed for better communication between healthcare providers, changed disease patterns, limited medical errors, and guaranteed proper documentation and protection of health information.

With the advent of personal computing, some healthcare organizations saw the modern age of healthcare coming a mile away and started working immediately, welcoming the introduction of health information systems and integrating them quickly into their hospitals and medical facilities.

Other organizations weren't so keen on the change. They had comfortably sailed along the River Routine with no desire to leave the Zone of Status Quo, thank you very much. They certainly weren't interested in dealing with waterfalls, even as they saw they were hurtling toward the Zone of Disruption! Despite the best efforts of the healthcare system, EMRs were no longer an "opt in" kind of change. Due to their clear advantages, accompanied by new legislation, a healthcare provider that didn't integrate an EMR was poised to experience huge losses and be out of government compliance.

This is where I came in.

I was a senior organizational-development consultant for a healthcare system, responsible for change-management support for the EMR implementation. As a change agent, it was my job to work with the Project Management team and other formal and informal leaders to ensure that the organization used sound change-management practices. While the rest of the organization was still in their Zone of Status Quo, the leadership team and I were laying the groundwork for the change.

For starters, enterprise-wide system changes like an EMR mean that lots of people have to learn to do their jobs very differently. It's hard to get excited about that, no matter what management says. A year before the intended go-live date, the Change Management team I led worked to uncover potential surprises—the kind that might derail teams, timelines, or budgets. This group of formal and informal leaders didn't try to talk people out of their concerns; we just took them all in, with the intent of building a change-management process that clarified the business case for change with our expanded understanding of constraints and barriers.

I learned an important lesson: Don't hesitate to prepare for change, even if it seems far away. Laying the groundwork for change requires understanding the landscape, with all its hills and valleys, and taking the long view. Your team will learn to lean into the change with you and will be more resilient throughout the process.

Seeing the Road Ahead

In the US, there are over a million accidents caused annually by deer collisions. According to State Farm Insurance, the odds of hitting a deer for US motorists are about 1 in 167—1 in 474 if you live in Hawaii, and 1 in 37 if you live in West Virginia.[18] Who knew these doe-eyed wildlife folk were such agents of chaos! And yet, how mindful we are of potential disruptions along the road ahead—be they deer or something else—says a lot about how we experience the Zone of Status Quo.

Use Your Peripheral Vision

When I was a teenager, I was driving late at night in Colorado. My dad, who was in the car with me, said, "Son, at this time of night there are always deer on the road in this area. Slow down, watch for the headlights' reflection in their eyes, and just expect that they will be there." Sure enough, minutes later, ahead on my right, just at the edge of the road, I saw several eyes and then

Curtis Bateman

the forms of the deer appeared in the darkness. But because I was ready, I didn't overreact. I calmly slowed the car and avoided the deer. It wasn't a big deal. But it could have been if I hadn't been expecting a deer to jump out in front of me.

Passengers in the car are likely doing other things—reading a book, watching a movie, texting, playing a game, or even napping. They are relying on you to be alert to all the risks as you drive. When you are alert and make minor adjustments well in advance, they may not even notice. However, when you are startled and react abruptly, passengers in the car are likely to feel helpless and scared by what is fully out of their control.

As Rita McGrath writes in *Seeing Around Corners: How to Spot Inflection Points in Business Before They Happen*, "I'm fond of an analogy to driving. When you can see far ahead, you can adjust your trajectory with a small move of the steering wheel; but when you see only after the inflection point is upon you, it requires a big jerk of the steering wheel. Put another way, when you can see an obstacle far down the road, you need to make a very small adjustment with your steering wheel. But when the obstacle is suddenly in front of your car, you have to quickly and drastically turn the wheel in a big, big way."[19]

If you're the leader with hands on the wheel and foot on the accelerator, you will experience the change differently from the people you lead (especially if you fail to see the change ahead and make a "big jerk" on the steering wheel). As a leader, you need to develop your scanning-ahead skill to prepare for potential changes. The "peripheral vision" you need can come from allowing a wide breadth of information to filter in—current news about your industry, anticipation of new government guidelines, feedback from clients, or employee observations you accumulate in your conversations. Use the Zone of Status Quo to look ahead and initiate small movements of the steering wheel. And remember, your team members are experiencing the ride differently—they're not in the driver's seat and don't have their hands or feet on the controls. The better we are at scanning the horizon for change, the less surprised we are by that change. (But take care that this doesn't become an anxious or paranoia-filled exercise. Scanning ahead should reduce fear, not heighten it.)

Scan, Ask, Act

There is an artful balance between being ignorant of unexpected change and being hyperfocused on finding it. Using our example of driving along the road with passengers in the car and being on the lookout for wildlife (a.k.a. unexpected change), consider three levels of change alertness and how they correspond to the Scan, Ask, Act behaviors:

Scan

Based on where you're driving and the time of year, the odds of encountering wildlife are low—but not zero. You don't want to be consumed by the thought of unexpected change, but you don't want to be caught off guard either.

Strategies

+ Use your peripheral vision. Keep a soft focus on the horizon, scanning for trends, patterns, or plans.
+ Use data to help predict what changes might occur.
+ Ask for others' perspectives.
+ Remain open to the eventuality of change without being consumed by it.

Ask

Where you're traveling (West Virginia versus Hawaii), the time of day (twilight), and the time of year (early winter) make for a significantly increased chance of encountering wildlife on the road. (Note that these are all data points referenced in the Relaxed Vigilance strategy, which could inform and prompt you to move to a more heightened alert.)

Strategies

- Narrow your focus as you watch for the telltale signs of the change you're expecting.
- Run "if/then" scenarios so you can preempt the change if it occurs.
- Ask for others' perspectives.
- Remain confident and ready to act.

Act

A deer (change) jumps onto the road ahead of you.

Strategies

- Assess what action to take (ideally, this is expedited by having run the "if/then" scenarios previously). If you're a passenger and not the driver, call out the danger ahead.
- Chart the best way forward given the useful information you have.
- Take quick and effective action.
- Stay in communication with everyone in the vehicle. They don't always know if a sudden jolt of the wheel is imminent.

Christi Phillips

Don't Go Over the Waterfall in the Dark

Earlier, I talked about laying the groundwork for change. This time, I want to talk about doing the early work of change. Prior to moving to Africa as a child, my family spent six months living in France. And like many people, I loved a good French croissant in the morning. Stopping at a *boulangerie* (bakery) for a warm, flaky croissant was the perfect way to start a day. But while it was the start of *my* day, it was definitely not the start of the day for the *boulangers* (bakers). While I had been sleeping, the bakers had been up all night, painstakingly preparing their wonderful pastries.

A leader preparing for change is somewhat like those bakers. While some people in the organization are comfortably "sleeping" through the Zone of Status Quo, change leaders are "up early," preparing for the change, putting things in place, so that when the change happens, when the people in the organization "wake up" to the change, leaders already have "breakfast" ready. They have prepared the vision, the communications plan, the systems, the training, the "nourishment" their people need to sustain them in their work as they go through the change.

During my career, every time I led a change initiative, I got a chance to participate in making my own version of croissants. Long before the rest of the organization knew much about the change, I helped leadership plan and prepare. We chose the system to roll out, we prepared training, we prepared messaging and communications, we put project management in place and, most importantly, we prepared to help, coach, and encourage our people throughout the change.

It wasn't that people in the organization were completely asleep. They heard that change was coming, because we talked with them while still laying the groundwork for change. They talked with each other and speculated on how the change might affect them. We knew they would need time to think about, discuss, and understand the change. Our team knew that keeping people in the dark, followed by a big reveal, is not the best way to prepare for change.

As a leader of change, do the hard work—the early work—long before the change, but don't keep your people in the dark about what you're cooking up.

Seeing Change in the Chaos

While our deer analogy has some legs to stand on (pun intended), leaders often experience change not as a solitary road at night, but as a cacophony of noise, moving parts, and ever-shifting landscapes. As it happens, air traffic controllers are experts at this kind of change awareness, seeing through the noise on the radar screen, tracking flights, and communicating with pilots and others. These change pros are responsible for overseeing a hundred thousand commercial flights around the globe daily.

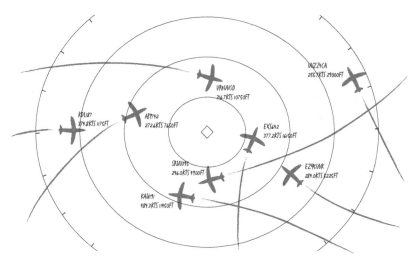

FIGURE 26: *Air Traffic Control Knows the Patterns.*

To turn a screen displaying a jumble of icons into a window on change, air traffic controllers:

+ **Know** the patterns. They're experts at understanding what the status quo should look like, even when it's crowded and full of moving parts.
+ **Filter** what they see and hear to spot the anomalies. Air traffic controllers use "peripheral vision," not so much to scan the darkness, but to see what deviates from the standard, normal, and expected.
+ **Prioritize** which planes to reroute and which to bring to the front of the line for landing.
+ **Act** by radioing the pilots and instructing them on what to do.

Whether your status quo looks like a river or a runway, effective leaders anticipate the change to come so they can prepare their teams and minimize the disruption.

Captain's Corner

Predict and Prepare for Change

Develop a culture in which your team members expect, anticipate, and prepare for change. There are three numbered questions listed below, with several examples (the bullet points) of how you might find the right answers. Use them as part of your "Predict and Prepare for Change" team meetings. (The bullet-point questions are only helpful as they relate to answering the numbered question above—what extra bullet points would you add?)

1. What change(s) might we see in the near future?
   - What trends do we notice in our industry or organization?
   - What current changes in technology, regulations, the market, etc., could affect us now or in the future?
   - What weaknesses or vulnerabilities should we shore up?
   - What developments do we see within our team and/or the organization?
   - Who inside the organization has their finger on the "pulse" of what's coming?
   - Who else might we ask, or what more could we do to help us better anticipate upcoming changes?
   - Who has faced a similar change (present-day or historical)? What did they do? What mistakes did they make? How can we avoid those mistakes?

2. Where could the change(s) lead?
   - What do these trends, potential changes, or developments suggest?
   - What are their consequences?
   - What are their potential benefits?
   - What might happen if we thoroughly anticipated possible changes?
   - How can we reduce the paranoia or anxiety of this change?

3. What can we do to prepare for the change(s) now?
   - How could we take advantage of the change?
   - What actions should we take now?
   - How can we continue to get our work done and not get distracted while looking for change?

Seeing Through the Two Lenses of Change

There are two "scopes" through which leaders view change while in the Zone of Status Quo. Think of one as a telescope and the other as a microscope. Leaders who effectively leverage the relative calm of the Zone of Status Quo use a change telescope to see faraway future events and probabilities. Like a telescope looking out past the horizon, the change telescope allows a leader to scan the darkness and focus hints of dim informational "light" to see a reorganization, merger, new product offering, international expansion, potential divestiture, leadership change, etc. This telescopic lens gathers information from multiple sources—as diverse as executive communication, strategic plans, institutional research, market analysis, stakeholder feedback, data trends, social media, and a favorite prognosticator's gut: to create a picture of what is coming and where the organization is going. The change telescope provides clarity around the *why* of the change and *what* the impact will be long before the team is disrupted. With this information, leaders can work to anticipate potential changes and act via skill acquisition, problem solving, finding resources, etc. This view allows leaders to prepare themselves, their teams, and the organization at large for change that may happen.

The change microscope focuses on the present (often amid the Zone of Disruption chaos). It provides magnified clarity about what just happened and what is happening, right after an unexpected (and often unwanted) change. The change microscope allows people to determine what the change can mean for individuals, the team, and the organization during the plummet into disruption's whitewater. This view of the change details quickly focuses the team's energy on creating a shared vision in the moment, versus the natural tendency to waste time figuring out whom to blame (thus the name of our parable, *Who Rocked the Boat?*). This view allows team members to quickly gain the clarity needed to decide to engage.

When we experience the effects of a change we've known was coming or that we proactively chose, we need clarity about what happened and why to get to the Point of Decision. When we are sucker punched by unexpected environmental change, we can use our change microscope to see the details of what happened, but it's usually up to us to create our own *why*. For instance, when the COVID-19 global pandemic put the world in change free fall, some organizations saw the *why* of the pandemic as a chance to tighten up their supply chains, right-size their office leases, and allow their employees a chance to prove work-from-home and hybrid models as tools to increase employee engagement and productivity. With the clarity they gained about *what* had happened, in combination with their own *why*, some organizations got busy leveraging this devastating change in ways that created incredible value (see Chapter Seven for a real-world example).

FIGURE 27: *Two Lenses of Change.*

Consider Anu Aga, who was suddenly facing a tremendous personal and professional change. Her husband, who was the head of Thermax, a multinational engineering company based in Pune, India, suddenly died of a heart attack. Anu took over the reins at the company at a difficult time, as the company was taking heavy losses.

Her husband had been a well-liked leader at the organization (which had been founded by his father), but he'd had difficulty holding people accountable and having tough conversations about performance. He had also branched out into several non-core businesses that were now performing very poorly and creating a drag on the main business.

When Anu took over (this was a family-owned business), she initially intended to make changes, but the board advised her to maintain the company in the Zone of Status Quo and run the business as her husband had. Then she received a letter from a disappointed shareholder, and she knew she needed to go with her instinct to make changes. But how was she to lead the company through these changes?

She first created a vision: "Restore Thermax and its stock to their old glory." With this vision, she felt she could lead the company through change: "A leader should be able to motivate, and more than motivate, create enthusiasm and passion; create a dream and make the team go toward it." To reach that vision, she determined to "make managers more accountable for results," and "exit low-profit, non-core businesses for focus," among other difficult changes.[20]

Within five years, she had righted the ship—the company was again profitable and even expanding its core business into the UK and the US. She had restored Thermax and its stock to their old glory. It had taken a lot of heavy lifting and tough decisions, but she successfully led the company through change. "A clear vision no doubt helped," Anu said.[21]

When announcing a change, leaders often fail to share a vision of the change. They just announce the change. In Anu Aga's case, she could have just announced, "We're going to make managers more accountable and exit some of our non-core businesses." But a change requires vision. Why would her people follow her if she had no vision?

To effectively communicate a compelling vision, you and your leaders must be able, at minimum, to answer these (and other) relevant questions:

1. *How* did we get here (to the edge of the waterfall)?
   a. *"In our rush to grow, we lost focus and diversified into too many non-core businesses. And I have some culpability in that as well."*
   b. *"We didn't hold ourselves accountable for results and we need to return to the discipline we've had around that."*
   c. *"In life, we all have some hubris and unjustified confidence in our own ideas. Frankly, that describes me as well, and I've been humbled. Now we all need to fine-tune our focus."*

2. *Where* are we going (the river ahead)?
   a. *"Let's talk courageously about our refined focus ahead and where we need everyone's greatest energy deployed."*
   b. *"That will require all of us to rise to a level of heightened focus and accountability, not just to each other and your teams, but also to your leader."*
   c. *"Ahead, we'll recapture our lost market share and again be the industry leader in our space."*

3. *Why* are we going there (to the other side)?

    a. *"In the past, our company had a 'value-based' approach, and we are going to again create that value for ourselves, our stockholders, and our customers."*

    b. *"The world's changed, and we need to discover new and better ways of doing business."*

    c. *"We're unwilling to accept our current diminished level of results."*

4. *What* will the journey be like (up the cliff)?

    a. *"I don't know all the twists and turns ahead. We'll have to try some new things, we'll certainly make some mistakes and learn from them, but we'll figure it out together."*

    b. *"When we experience setbacks—because, let's face it, this is going to be challenging—we'll have to reconnect to our what and why so we don't lose our resolve."*

Captain's Corner

Create a Compelling Case for Change

Once you've clarified how a change disruption came to be (if necessary), communicate the case for change to your team in a compelling, relevant way, so they catch the vision of it. Draft and share a memorable story your team can understand and easily retell about where the team/organization is going, why they are going there, and what the journey will look like. Use prompts like the following:

1. Describe the problem or opportunity targeted by the change.
   - "We have been struggling with..."
   - "We have been planning to..."

2. Describe how the change solves the problem or creates the opportunity.
   - "The change we are making is..."
   - "So we've decided to..."

3. Share the benefits of the change for the team and the organization.
   - "When we make this change successfully, we will..." [Describe the outcomes it will achieve or opportunities it will create.]

- "If we succeed with this change, we will prevent/solve/overcome..." [Describe the problems it will solve or issues it will resolve.]

4. Share the challenges of the change (be as transparent as you can). Share any bad news they should know (information that is legal and appropriate to share).
   - "I know this means we will..."
   - "When we make the change, we will have to..."

5. Share initial ideas on how to address the challenges together.
   - "I think we can handle these challenges by..."
   - "We have overcome challenges like this in the past, such as..."

6. Summarize what you are moving from and what you are moving to.
   - "As we make this change, we will move from... to..." [Be as specific as you can about required behavior or procedural changes, as well as the new outcomes the changes will need to produce. There should be multiple "from-to" statements focusing on behaviors, actions, and results that should change.]

Note: As you prepare the Case for Change, reflect on your level of commitment. You won't be effective in leading your team through the change if you're not fully committed to it.

Aligning Dialogue to Cascading Change Visions

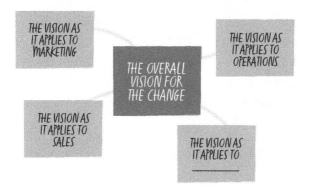

FIGURE 28: *Supporting the Overarching Vision.*

Leaders tend to want to use a bull-horn approach to announcing change, when what is needed is creating dialogue around vision at every level and within each function of an organization.

Except in very small organizations, you will have several functional visions that support the overarching enterprise vision. For example, an organizational vision around growth will likely be supported by an HR vision around employee engagement, a Product Development vision around new product innovation, and a Sales/Marketing vision around speed of market adoption for new products. Leaders tend to want to use a bullhorn approach to announcing change, when what is needed is creating dialogue around vision at every level and within each function of an organization.

This cascading vision continues all the way to the department and even team level. Think of it like this: You call an "all-hands" meeting and announce a significant change. You only have time to take a couple of questions, so the graphic artist asks one. You don't really understand the question, because that's not your world, so you give a general statement that doesn't really answer what they asked. Meanwhile, the salespeople and Customer Support team members are looking at the time, eager to get out of there. They don't care about the question asked by the graphic artist, as that's not their world either. But to the graphic artist, that question is vital. It *is* their world.

Alternatively, what if, as a leader, you created a vision and fostered dialogue around supporting visions at various levels within the different functions of the organization? In this way, the questions, suggestions, complaints, fears, and excitement that affect individuals within a specific part of the organization can be truly heard and authentically addressed. It may also mean pulling the right experts into the discussion as well—your graphic artist deserves an answer to their question, even if you're not the one who's able to address it.

Leveling Up for Change

Effectively moving through change is a skill that can be learned. As a leader, you want to build change "muscle memory" into your team so that their reactions can be instinctual and automatic. In essence, you want them to "level up" their mindsets and skillsets around change. The more you're prepared to coach your team through the change, the more likely it is this can happen. Even though the Change Model defines four zones, change is an iterative process. After climbing out of the ravine (and hopefully innovating as a result), you return to the Zone of Status Quo, but at a new level. Now you're not just scanning ahead—the Zone of Status Quo provides the perfect opportunity to capitalize on the lessons learned from navigating the previous change to build more resilience, inspire more confidence, and deepen engagement in your team.

Curtis Bateman

How to Coach Change "Newbies" to Level Up

On a long stretch of deserted road, my wife and I were teaching my son how to drive a car. After my son took his seat behind the wheel, we went through all the controls for the car, adjusted the mirrors, talked about our strategy for getting on the highway, determined safe speeds, and discussed what to do if something unexpected happened. He then pulled out onto the sleepy two-lane highway.

It didn't go very well.

My son just didn't yet have the skills needed to drive on the highway. We had only practiced driving in parking lots and quiet neighborhood streets. The highway was throwing so much new information at him that he started only paying attention to the thing I was talking about—like the dashboard instead of the road!

Eventually, my wife suggested we pull over so I could drive and talk my son through what I was doing. So we switched places, and I went through the same process of adjusting the mirrors and controls. But then I paused. Instead of relying on my instincts and reflexes from years of driving, I described every single step I was going through. As I pulled out on the road, I explained, "I'm checking my left mirror, and this is what I'm looking for... Now I'm checking my rear-view mirror, and this is what I'm looking for... Now that I can see it's clear, I'm looking ahead and noticing there's one car off in the distance... I'm switching on my turn signal and accelerating onto the highway."

I went into detail about the various things I no longer thought consciously about as an experienced driver. I explained how hard I was pushing on the gas pedal and when I was easing off. I pointed out my glances at the rear-view mirror and what I was looking for. I made it explicit when I was looking ahead to see oncoming traffic, checking my side mirrors, glancing at my speedometer, reading the speed limit and other traffic signs and signals, checking that the lane was clear in preparation to pass another car, checking my blind spots, watching for animals and children at play, looking out for possible road hazards, and so on—all the driving behaviors that had become automatic and instinctual.

Describing every single movement, minor detail, habit, and reflex associated with driving reminded me of the responsibilities of leaders who are ushering their teams through change. As the leader, you are teaching your novices to build awareness around all of what's in front of them, without tackling or fixing all the minute issues. After all, the goal is for your people to get behind the wheel and drive, not watch you from the passenger seat. What feels instinctual for those with experience can be daunting for newbie team members, who can easily become overwhelmed by the number of things to pay attention to. Such team members are likely to hyperfocus on what's immediately in front of them, missing the bigger picture and ending up getting disrupted by something they couldn't foresee.

As a leader, it takes deliberate work to develop the reflexes, patterns, and behaviors required to navigate change. Eventually, our team's change reflexes will become intuitive as members build change muscles and don't have to commit nearly the same amount of mental energy to navigate the change journey.

Identifying the Skills, Knowledge, and Tools Needed for Change

Executives need frontline leaders to summarize and communicate the gaps in skills, knowledge, or tools necessary for the change to succeed.

Leaders have the responsibility to shape an organization's reaction to change. They need to foresee and respond to change, but they also need to frame the change within the bigger picture. As the organization starts to understand the change, each of the various parts of the organization will need to map current skills, knowledge, and tools to what will be asked of them. Some parts of the organization might need to ramp up certain capabilities to navigate the change successfully. These areas could include technical skills as well as soft skills. Other parts of the organization may be just fine with their current skill levels. They might need to know more, however, or adopt new tools.

Executives need frontline leaders to summarize and communicate the gaps in skills, knowledge, or tools necessary for the change to succeed. That's why the communication plan needs to feature two directions—bottom to top, top to bottom. This means moving from a broadcast message to dialogue. After a leader announces a change, and that becomes a functional discussion at the team level, gaps/needs/questions/resources/constraints will surface. This feedback should move back to leadership so the details that arise from a frontline perspective can help them further refine, or even adjust, the change strategy. A leader who announces, "We all need to learn new things because of this change—starting with *me*," will show a level of vulnerability and honesty that builds trust and helps team members know their leader is "in it" with them.

Andy Cindrich

Learn the Ropes **Before** *the Storm Hits*

The Zone of Status Quo provides an opportunity for training. It's during the calm *before* the storm, or as we've mentioned earlier, in the space "between the waves," that new skills can be learned, and teams can become better prepared to meet the challenges ahead. But many leaders fail to allocate budget and time for people development.

I see it all the time. When I consult with clients, helping them prepare for a change, I often encourage them to take the opportunity afforded them, in this time of relative calm, to level up their teams. I ask leaders if they would prefer to pull their people offline for training and development *now* or when they are in the throes of change disruption. Personally, I'd rather my crew learn how to work the sails in calm waters than in the middle of a storm, when the waves are crashing across the bow of the ship.

For those leaders who don't take advantage of the gift of the pre-storm calm, they miss an opportunity to invest in developing their people, inoculating them against overtures from competitors or headhunters or better preparing them to succeed with the change ahead. The constant state of change means a storm is always brewing on the horizon. The most effective change leaders train their crew to be pros at navigating stormy seas, and I'd rather they develop those skills in relatively calm waters—especially when I'm on board too!

Captain's Corner

Providing Opportunities for Growth in the Zone of Status Quo

If you're in the calm of the Zone of Status Quo, ask your people the following questions:

- Are you recovering and recharging, or are you stagnating?
- What do you see as your most important training and development needs?
- What do you need to learn to achieve your most important goals?
- Are there any obstacles to your development that I can help you with?

From the Zone of Status Quo to the Zone of Disruption

Now that the River Routine has run its course, there's nothing left to do but go over the waterfall and experience the turmoil and confusion of the Zone of Disruption.

CHAPTER SIX

The Zone of Disruption

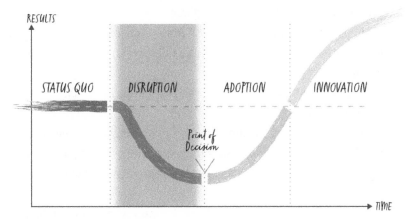

FIGURE 29: *The Zone of Disruption.*

Clarify the Change

The Zone of Disruption is the plummet over a change waterfall. Results fall, and team members can be thrown off by the chaos and emotion of the disruption. The leader's job is to help each individual answer for themselves:

- *What's* changing?
- *Why* is it changing?
- *How* will it affect me?

Notice that these are different from the questions in the Zone of Status Quo, which focus on the nature of the change and the path forward. In the Zone of Disruption, things are personal, and emotions are often running high. Effective change leaders address the impact of the change *for every individual* on their team.

Reactions in the Zone of Disruption

The captain in *Who Rocked the Boat?* worked to clarify what was happening as they plummeted over the waterfall and crashed below. Leaders battle insecurity with information. This is essential because of the way the crew reacts:

"I told you this would happen! We're goners!" *Quit* shouted above the fray.

"We should have dropped the anchor!" *Resist* exclaimed.

"Oh my!" *Wait* cried out, clinging to the rails and terrified of how much worse things could get.

Move whooped with delight and relished the adrenaline rush.

Minimize kept quiet.

Each crew member was feeling the disruption differently. The captain, however, had to stay cool and calm throughout. The need for pastoral care (a British term that captures the shepherding sentiment well) in the Zone of Disruption is high.

> **Leaders battle insecurity with information.**

After the crew survives the fall, *Quit* moans: "But why did we have to take *this* route? There are lots of other waterways out there. Whose crazy idea was it to take the river with the waterfall?" Despite the temptation to figure out who's to blame (thus the parable's title, *Who Rocked the Boat?*), it's a distraction from the three questions that matter in the Zone of Disruption: *what* is changing, *why* is it changing, and *how* will it impact me? Consider how the captain moved through the three questions:

- *What is changing?* "The waterfall wreaked havoc on our poor ship and left us bruised and broken."
- *Why is it changing?* "No river will ever stay constant, so waterfalls will always be a part of the journey."
- *How will it impact me?* "I know this is not what any of us expected, but we'll figure it out together."

The crew comes up with different answers for how to proceed. And they do so through the lens of what they're *willing* and *wanting* to do. This is a very human response to change, and the captain has quite a bit of work to do to rally everyone together and move them to the Point of Decision. Change requires leadership and not necessarily consensus. While everyone is invited to take part in brainstorming solutions, the captain keeps the crew focused on the larger objective: "Our charge is to take *Results* and her cargo to the mountains and port beyond—both of which are on higher ground." Despite the disruption of going over the waterfall, leaders often have to remind their teams that their larger jobs and goals *haven't* changed.

Clarity Moves You Past the Zone of Disruption

Lieutenant Hiroo Onoda desperately needed clarity. But it took an agonizing twenty-nine years to happen, and that's a long time to be stuck in the Zone of Disruption.

Onoda was a Japanese soldier sent to an island in the Philippines during World War II with specific instructions from his commanding officer, Major Yoshimi Taniguchi: "You are absolutely forbidden to die by your own hand. It may take three years, it may take five, but whatever happens, we'll come back for you. Until then, so long as you have one soldier, you are to continue to lead him. You may have to live on coconuts. If that's the case, live on coconuts! Under no circumstances are you [to] give up your life voluntarily."[22]

Onoda was extremely faithful to this command. After Allied forces captured the island from the Japanese, he and other soldiers broke into small groups of four to disappear into the jungle and continue fighting a guerrilla war. These cells of Japanese soldiers were killed off or captured, until eventually just Onoda's group remained. They became very skilled at living off what they could forage or steal from local farms, as they continued their guerrilla efforts.

Then the big change happened—the war ended. Onoda and the other Japanese soldiers, cut off from communications with the Japanese military, were unaware of the change. They continued doing what they had been doing. Over time, people began to realize that Onoda's group didn't know the war had ended. In October 1945, local islanders, tired of having their farms raided for food, put out leaflets declaring, "The war ended August 15. Come down from the mountains!"

"Propaganda!" Onoda and the others decided. They didn't buy any of the messages made by locals, the leaflets dropped from B-17s, or even petitions from fellow Japanese military and government officials to get them to come out of their hiding places. *There was no way the war could have ended,* they thought. *If the war was over, Japan would have won, and they would come get us.* And because, in their minds, there was no way Japan could lose, the war must still be going on.

After five years, one member of the group, Yuichi Akatsu, slipped away and surrendered. Several years later, Soichi Shimada was killed in a shootout with local fishermen. After twenty-seven years, Kinshichi Kozuka was killed by a Philippine police patrol.

Twenty-seven years!

People had long assumed that Onoda was dead, but when Kozuka was killed, they thought Onoda might still be alive and continuing the fight. Several searches for Onoda failed. Then, two years later in 1974, an adventurous Japanese man, Norio Suzuki, set out to find the missing soldier. Incredibly, he found Onoda, still alive and living a hand-to-mouth existence deep in the jungle. For nearly three decades, Onoda had followed his original orders. Norio Suzuki realized that, in addition to finding the elusive soldier, he needed to provide Onoda with clarity that the world had changed around him:

- *What:* He gave Onoda the details about how the war ended.
- *Why:* He shared the reasons why the war ended.
- *Impact on Onoda:* He told Onoda that he no longer needed to fight; he could go home.

Suzuki nearly convinced Onoda to accept the change, but Onoda needed one last bit of clarity—he needed to hear these things from his commanding officer. Onoda replied, "I am a soldier and remain true to my duties." He would only return if he was officially relieved. So Suzuki returned to Japan, found Onoda's former commander, Taniguchi (who was now working in a book-store), and the two of them returned to the Philippines. The former military commander formally relieved Onoda of his duties and clarified that the war had indeed ended. Finally, after three decades, Onoda chose to accept the change, and they returned to Japan together.[23]

Incredible and nearly unbelievable?

Yes.

Factually true?

Yes.

In the face of the most profound change and getting stalled in the Zone of Disruption (even for decades!), *clarity* is the skill for moving to the Point of Decision and beyond.

 # Captain's Corner

Clarify the Specifics of the Change

Change disrupts regular, habitual routines. It can create chaos, fear, and insecurity in teams, causing a dip in results. To reduce your team's fears, use the table below to get crystal clear on as many as possible of the specific results and actions they must move *from* and move *to*. Elicit your team's ideas as well, since they are closest to the work affected by the change.

MOVING FROM	MOVING TO
Before the change, the team was responsible for achieving these results:	With the change, the team is now responsible for achieving these results:
1.	1.
2.	2.
3.	3.
4.	4.
5.	5.
6.	6.
7.	7.
8.	8.
To achieve the old results, the team used to take these actions:	To achieve success with the change, the team now needs to take these actions:
1.	1.
2.	2.
3.	3.
4.	4.
5.	5.
6.	6.
7.	7.
8.	8.

Envision, Don't Just Convey

Change, even change for the better, creates disruption—which means it's a place you don't want to stay very long. You can't skip the zone, but you can reduce the time you're in it. How to get out? Get clarity on what's happening, why it's happening, and how it affects your team. This doesn't mean you have a boilerplate answer that you send as an email. An effective leader will tailor the message to each individual and to how they're reacting in the moment. Put another way, a leader must envision the impact of the change on each team member and resist conveying a stock answer. Instead, this is an ongoing dialogue that leads to taking ownership of how your team will choose to react (the Point of Decision). Simply *telling* team members how to implement a change often creates pushback; people don't feel heard or understood. As a result, engagement and productivity will suffer. Like Lieutenant Onoda's commander, you may be inadvertently keeping your people stuck in the Zone of Disruption. Sure, you may send out emails or a letter from the CEO to inform everyone, but such "leaflets" dropped from metaphorical airplanes simply convey a message that won't necessarily be well received or even believed. When it comes to communicating through the Zone of Disruption, ask yourself: "Am I just blanketing everyone with leaflets?" People need dialogue and the chance to ask questions before they can become invested enough to take ownership of the change.

People need dialogue and the chance to ask questions before they can become invested enough to take ownership of the change.

But what if you *are* that executive leader or CEO? Obviously, you can't tailor an announcement to each member of the organization. In the previous chapter, we discussed how the cascading change message can be an effective way of making change feel relevant and connected to individuals across varied departments and teams.

Which is to say, the CEO's message may firmly set up the values behind and objectives for a change, with leader-to-leader communication to connect that message to departmental strategies, followed by communication at the team level to talk about tactics and implementation. The point is, regardless of how your organization is structured, the temptation to carpet-bomb the companywide email account is unlikely to produce the change engagement you're looking for. Connect and align the messages, but make them appropriate and meaningful at each organizational stratification.

It's the leader's responsibility in the Zone of Disruption to make the change coherent and comprehensible. Your job isn't to force people into the change, shame them into change, or tell them to just "embrace change." Your job is to provide clarity for the decision—their job is to decide whether to engage.

Curtis Bateman

Cascading Messaging at a Call Center

Picture this: You run a call center with over five thousand employees, and you realize the next step to improving your client satisfaction involves a significant change that only works if every person and every role in the call center engages. Your message needs to make it to everyone, and they need to be aligned to the new behaviors. So, what do we often do? We tell them. And when that doesn't work, we tell them again and again. Usually the volume increases with each telling. We call this the "MORE" button. If it didn't work the first time, hit the MORE button and say it again. Leaders need a different way when leading large-scale changes, a way that creates *alignment* and *engagement* across the organization. Here are three easy steps to help with that:

1. The change sponsor creates a "Case for Change." This is a simple one-page message on *why* this change, *what* led to it, and the story of how this will lead to something better. Include a few Moving From and Moving To statements at the end to illustrate the new behaviors, actions, or results.

2. The change sponsor asks each of the leaders to develop their own change story from the "Case for Change." Leaders then tell the story to their people as it aligns with the team's responsibilities.

3. Allow the discussion about the change story to create dialogue both up and down the organizational structure. Being part of the story and having a voice creates engagement around the change.

Start the Change Story at the Beginning

Imagine you and a friend go to a movie. But you arrive a half hour after the movie has started. You take your seat just as the hero announces, "All right, people, we know what we need to do and why it matters, so let's do it!"

Because you arrived late, you have no idea what's happening, who the characters are, or what challenge they're facing. Instead of rooting for the success of the mission (you don't know enough of the backstory to be invested), you're playing catch-up for the rest of the film and trying to work things out. This is not unlike how your team members can feel when they take their seat in the theater of change. *You* have likely been involved for some time—you know the change backstory, including the why, the players, and the stakes. But your team can feel like they've arrived late—they know something is about to happen, but they're mostly confused, annoyed, and uninvested in the outcome.

As a leader, you have the chance to push pause and catch everyone up. This is essential, because without knowing the full change story, your team will try to "figure it out" on their own, often telling negative stories and assuming bad intent. Don't let that happen. Create a safe place for dialogue where you can answer questions and resolve issues before signaling the projectionist to roll the film.

Andy Cindrich

A Change "Sad Lib"

I'm going to share a story with you in a fill-in-the-blank format, like the Mad Libs word game (but I'm calling this a Sad Lib), drawn from actual events. As I relate this, think of your team and how a change didn't go very well. Fill in the blanks from your experience. Of course, your experience won't map exactly to this, but you'll get the idea.

A few years ago, I consulted with a/an (industry) company going through a change. A particular leader responded (adverb ending in -ly) to the team's change reactions. The leader only provided (a number less than 10) percent of the clarity they needed to reach the Point of Decision. The company was in the middle of a/an (adjective describing size) change to (noun), which resulted in a/an (adjective) impact on the team's results, dropping their results from (level) to (level).

The team's reactions to the disruption varied from (emotion) to (emotion). Many on the team didn't want to engage in the change because of (noun). To feel comfortable enough to engage in the change, they needed to know (noun) and to be sure (noun) wouldn't happen. With that clarity, they could reach a decision. But things weren't going well. To me, it seemed their chance of reaching a decision was one in (number larger than a million).

I advised them that they wouldn't reach the Point of Decision, where the team could engage with the change, unless they got (synonym for clarity) around the *what*, the *why*, and the impact on their team.

But rather than providing the clarity the team needed, the leader berated them for (verb ending in -ing). That pushed the team further from the Point of Decision. Now they were more cautious and (antonym of decisive). Their results dropped even further. In trying to force people out of the Zone of Disruption through fear and (noun), this leader was actually prolonging the disruption.

I worked further with this leader, coaching them to provide clarity and trust and inspire the team, but this leader chose to ignore best practices and instead moved to (a tactic that never works). That didn't work, and emotions ran high. Next, this leader moved to (another tactic that also never works). That got results... the wrong results: a mess people didn't want.

I've found that effective leaders do the opposite of what this leader did. They:

- Acknowledge that results dip in the Zone of Disruption.
- Reject the idea that results will always be lower (a new, lower status quo).
- Recognize each team member's reaction to change.
- Don't escalate by negatively reacting to their reactions. Rather, they let each reaction help others understand what clarity they need to provide that person to help them get to the Point of Decision.
- Work with the team to gather/create/provide the clarity needed to decide to engage.
- Invite them to make and own their decision

Captain's Corner

Getting to Clarity Sooner

To help your people get to the clarity they need around a change, consider asking the following questions in your next 1-on-1:

- In your own words, what is going on? What is this change? Could you describe the change to me?
- Why is this change happening? What's the background? What led to this change, and why are we doing this?
- How might this change impact you? How do you think it might impact our team and organization?
- What's your reaction to all this?
- What clarification, background, or information do you need to make sense of the change?

Why Change Can Feel Like an Escape Room

Think of the Zone of Disruption as an "escape room" (a popular game in which participants enter a room where they discover clues, use logic, and accomplish given tasks to complete the game and "escape"). The game originated with Flash games for web browsers in the early 2000s, then continued to physical locations in the USA, Japan, and Hungary, and then spread throughout the world. By the end of 2019, it was estimated that there were over 50,000 escape rooms worldwide.[24]

In an escape room, the players are eager to figure out how to get out of the room. At first, they likely don't even know what they're looking for. The information needed to get free is not readily apparent: there isn't a checklist on the wall that says, "Understand this and that. Do these things in this order." Each group must figure it out on their own. So the players just start—they open drawers, decode clues, and look for patterns and anomalies. Each player brings a unique perspective, insight, and approach to the challenge.

So, what does clarity look like in the Zone of Disruption? We can't tell you. Seriously. Every Zone of Disruption brings different clarification needs. Some changes are complex. Some are straightforward. Some are counterintuitive. Reactions vary. Your team may be 50 percent *Wait* and 50 percent *Move*. You may have 80 percent *Quits* and the rest *Resist*. Perhaps you have a few ready to *Move* but are afraid to confront a bunch who *Resist*. You may have 100 percent eager to *Move*, but they don't know where to go. Your team may disagree with the vision. Or some members of your team may be on board but feel like they don't have the capability to handle the change. They may have unanswered questions: "Will I lose my job?" "Is this change up for negotiation?" "Will I have different responsibilities?" "Why didn't you tell us about this sooner?" Each member of your team may have different clarity needs.

Also, the change may not go the way you, the leader, expected it to go. Despite planning and preparation, changes often go off the rails, and that can feel like a gut punch to your well-intentioned plans.

Every escape room is different, and so every "escape" will be different. It's as if each member of your team is in an individual escape room and needs to find their own way. For some, it will be easy to find the door and just open it. For others, it will be more challenging. But for each person, there is a way out. You just have to help them find it. You need to be emotionally agile and flexible in your expectations as to how each team member may opt in to the change at their own pace. Meet each person where they are. Some need more hand-holding than others. Work together with your team members to gather information, look for clues, use logic, figure out what's relevant and what's not, make connections between seemingly unrelated things, use your intuition, and get creative.

Once your team members have the clarity they need, they can open the door at the Point of Decision and walk through to the Zone of Adoption. And while we wish there were a clarity checklist hanging on the escape-room wall, there isn't. But you and your team are okay without one. Because having a framework for change means you can handle any escape room that comes your way.

Sharing Lessons Learned to Expedite Change (EMR Adoption, Part Three)

Christi Phillips

Let's jump back into the massive change I was involved in: helping hospitals transition from paper to electronic-based records. I got to see firsthand how it disrupted people. There now had to be records of everything. For example, in between surgeries, those who cleaned the medical devices and instruments had to capture everything they did. They had to enter each piece into the system in a certain way, each tong and tweezer and scalpel, the anesthesia machines. Everything needed to be recorded as being clean. Nurses needed to keep records when they were patient-facing: when they gave medications, when they took the patient's vital signs, and when they took notes to hand off to nurses on the next shift. People who cleaned the rooms didn't love the change to the electronic system. Physicians didn't love the system. Many had to change the way they worked. Early on, we assessed all sorts of risks; we anticipated how people would react (both individually and collectively), and we prepared to guide each person with their somewhat predictable reaction to where we wanted them to go. Our goal was not to be surprised by the dip, not to be surprised by the reactions, and to be ready.

Our change-management plan included creating learning teams who would share lessons learned and provide feedback about what wasn't working so that issues could be addressed and corrected. And our plan ensured the measurement of our progress to further clarify the desired end state, and to ensure the momentum would continue. Like the escape-room example, this meant different solutions for different individuals, surfaced through ongoing dialogue and feedback, and shared up and down the line so that we could capitalize on the lessons learned and make the necessary adjustments. And while not everyone "made it out," so to speak, a large majority of the organization found their way through and to the exit (i.e., the Point of Decision).

Clarify by Switching From Monologue to Dialogue

When change happens, do you *hear* the people you lead? Part of hearing how change impacts your people is listening for things that may seem insignificant to you but may be important to them. Listen for what they value.

Curtis Cassel, a well-respected architect renowned for his firm's success in public-school design, was stunned: "In my career, I had never lost a referendum campaign for a school district. I had confidence. I had the reputation. I had the support of the school board president." What Cassel didn't have was the backing of the voters. Far from it. Voters were mad. The referendum to fund building upgrades throughout the district looked to be going down in flames.

Cassel's firm, TRi, an architectural firm, had planned for the first public-engagement meeting to be uneventful, with fewer than 250 people in attendance. Over five hundred people showed up, much more than the room could accommodate. Cassel described the situation: "Our presentation of the 'future of education' was disrupted multiple times. Voices got loud. Tensions rose. I took my typical approach of walking into the crowds to allow dissenters a voice with a microphone. It wasn't working. Anger grew. I attempted to shift their focus to a 'no tax increase' bond issue. They weren't buying it."

Why weren't they buying it?

It quickly became apparent that the priorities being presented by their firm were diametrically opposed to what this group of voters (parents) felt needed to be addressed. A near-irreparable chasm opened, and no amount of "telling" was going to close it and bring consensus. Cassel realized the community needed to connect and openly talk about something they valued: safety. Many of the school district properties hadn't been improved much in fifty years, so there were major safety concerns. "It was to become about safety. Safety for children..." The focus went to what repairs and where. Cassel shared the experience of the next meeting: "The next public engagement was very different, although the tone started off where we left it.... We revealed what schools rarely want constituents to see: shocking photos of exposed electrical wires, nonfunctioning toilets, code violations, broken stairs, flooded basements, and asbestos-containing materials. We discussed the lack of proper air conditioning and the impact on children. Nonconforming areas of the building for accessibility and discriminatory conditions for those in wheelchairs were illustrated. We presented information slowly. It sunk in and was sobering.

"We then asked for all those same, hostile people to help us. Help us prioritize the ways to spend their money. What was most important to them—removal of hazardous materials, air quality, code upgrades, plumbing? Where would we spend their funds—at each school site, a few buildings at a time? What is most fair when you only have a third of the funds needed?"

Cassel shifted from monologue to dialogue. He brought the parents into the conversation.

As a leader, to help your people reach the end of the Zone of Disruption and approach the Point of Decision, clarify the Case for Change through the lens of shared values. Finding the intersection of what the organization values, what you as a leader value, and what your team values can be a powerful tool for engagement.

Marché Pleshette

Finding the Intersection of Values

I have always felt there is a social and psychological part of change that is ignored when leaders are responsible for implementing a change. Often leaders are so laser-focused on the change goal and a logistical path to getting there that they sometimes forget that change is really about people. Change cannot implement itself. It takes human beings, each of whom has their own goals, fears, personalities, preferences, histories, insights, and values. It's unlikely an organizational change will line up perfectly with each person's goals and values, but it's very possible to find points of inter-section. That is one of the greatest strategies you can leverage as a change leader—to find those points of interconnecting values that enable team members to see how the proposed change might be mutually beneficial. It is an act/expression of win-win thinking.

For starters, get an understanding of what's important to your people. That's not something you can learn in an instant, and it should not be reserved just for change. Get to know team members over time and learn what they value by listening to, observing, and dialoguing with them. Only through this can we understand what motivates them and where they might more fully connect to all you're missioned to do.

Know that your people are also getting a feel for what's important to you. They form an opinion of the company as a whole by sizing up the leadership team and learning how coworkers and operations func-tion. Employees hear what the company says it values—as captured in vision and mission statements and the things leadership says—but they are quite observant of the difference between what's said and what's done. They are, perhaps subconsciously, assessing whether you, the organization, and the team are in alignment with them.

In Chapter Four, I spoke about giving team members a compelling case for change. What makes the case compelling? It's when what the company values and what your people value intersect. It's when leaders can clearly articulate those intersections of value and invite people to opt in to the change. Of course, it's always important to have integrity, but during times of change, when employees may more readily scrutinize the actions and intentions of leaders, it's especially important to show your people that they can trust and believe in those intersections of value.

Recently, during a FranklinCovey client work session, an individual expressed dismay with the irony that the organization boasted of "respect, inclusion, trust, and accountability as their core values," yet this individual's team had been told that there would soon be a reorganization but given no additional insight regarding how it would work and how they might be supported if they were impacted. She articulated aloud during the work session that she couldn't be fully mentally present because she had no idea if, by the end of the week, she would have a job. During a conversation over the break, she said, "I've given a lot to this company. Even if I am laid off, it would be satisfying to know that there's a severance or plan to see me through for a while. Instead, they just scare us with the fact that any one of us could lose our jobs and have nothing." She was angry that the organization was not aligned with their expressed values and was disappointed that her values didn't seem to carry much weight with the company.

Beyond transparency during a reorganization or a financial benefit in another organizational change, maybe recognition is important to a team member who is considering their part in executing change. If recognition is a value of team members, incorporate it! If it's personal words of gratitude they desire for their contribution, do that. Whatever the values of your people, they are also potential motivators—so learn what's important. It's no secret, post-COVID, that people's values have been massively reassessed and reprioritized. As a result, it's a crucial job of any leader not only to understand them, but to provide a heightened sense of an individualized style of leadership to better identify and connect to those intersections. There are feelings, behaviors, and actions that follow. Discuss openly and honestly what's important to you and company leadership, then find the common ground. When they see how, in some ways, your values, goals, and desires align with theirs, you show them the possibility of mutual benefit and stay present to talk it through, and then you will see the sweet reward of having supported a team member who chose to opt in. That's a win-win!

Getting to the Point of Decision When Emotions Are Strong and the Stakes Are High

When a change is imposed on us, it's our human reaction to push back and resist. Leaders guiding their team members through change will likely experience this, especially if there are strong emotions involved or if the stakes feel high. Sometimes tragedy strikes—terrible things happen, and we come face to face with heartbreak. This is simply a reality of life, both personally and professionally. Our premise, however, is that even when a change involving high stakes or high emotions is imposed, every single choice someone can make will help them regain some measure of control and influence over how that change affects them. It may feel like we're bereft of choices, but an effective leader can help coach a team member to find some level of empowerment, no matter how small, to move forward. It may mean you need to slow down and take a little extra time with them, but it's an investment well worth making.

> *...every single choice someone can make will help them regain some measure of control and influence over how that change affects them.*

Captain's Corner

Clarify by Connecting to Values So Your Team Can Opt In

In 1-on-1s or in group meetings, ask every member of your team to answer the questions below. If your team struggles to answer them, talk with them to make the value proposition clear. If you're in a high-stakes situation or emotions are running high, you may need more time helping team members deal with their reactions to the change and working through what they are thinking, feeling, and doing.

- What are we thinking, feeling, and doing as a result of this change?
- What's the impact on us?
- What could success look like in this new scenario?
- What are the obstacles that stand in the way of success?

If your team needs more information to connect what they value to the change, reflect on and answer the following questions:

- What are the values of the organization? (It's likely these are captured and shared somewhere.)
- How do those values inform the objectives of the change?
- What are the values of your team?
- What are the values of your individual team members? (If you can't answer this, safely explore it during your next 1-on-1.)
- What values align at the individual, team, and organizational level?
- Knowing those shared values, how can you clarify through the Zone of Disruption by anchoring your message to those values?
- How will doing the above make it more likely that your team members will opt in to the change?

Crossing Through the Point of Decision

Having done the work in the Zone of Adoption to prepare your team to engage with and take ownership of what they can control in the change (and let go of what they can't), it's time to cross through the Point of Decision together.

CHAPTER SEVEN

The Point of Decision

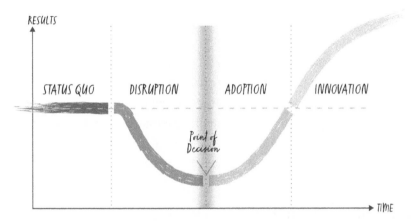

FIGURE 30: *The Point of Decision.*

Gaining Commitment to Opt In and Own the Change

The Point of Decision is the doorway between the Zone of Disruption and the Zone of Adoption. It's where your team's thinking shifts from *You're doing this to me,* to *I get what's changing; I understand the why and the value of it; I understand what it means to me and I choose to be a part of the change.*

It can be tempting at the Point of Decision to choose to go back to the way things were working before and simply accept lower results.

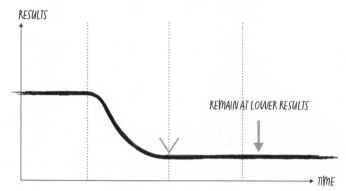

FIGURE 31: *Remain at Lower Results.*

After all, a change happened, and the impact on results was outside of your control. This makes it enticing to "double down" on old behaviors, hoping they'll eventually pay off. But rarely will that be sufficient, and the business world is replete with stories of organizations that, trapped in the Zone of Disruption, stuck to "business as usual" and ended up paying the price (sometimes as high as going out of business).

Reactions at the Point of Decision

Consider how *Who Rocked the Boat?* describes the captain and crew's experience at the Point of Decision:

> *The current carried Results to a sandy beach where they dropped anchor and disembarked. As they gathered on the shore, they noticed how the sand pulled and tugged at their boots. It was slow moving here, as if the place wanted to keep them stuck. The captain said, "I think we can rest here for a bit, but we don't want to stay too long. Let's decide what to do and get moving."*

All the clarifying work done in the Zone of Disruption paves the way for the team to now opt in and take ownership of the decision themselves.

The big idea here is that there's a real

temptation for those going through disruptive change to stay put. While the captain was empathic to the toll taken by going over the waterfall, it remained a leadership responsibility to guide the crew to a decision and a commitment to act on that decision. The clarifying work done in the Zone of Disruption paves the way for the team to now opt in and take ownership of the decision themselves—a key personal investment that will yield dividends during the hard climb in the Zone of Adoption.

 # Captain's Corner

Assess Commitment to Change

Observe your team in their work, in 1-on-1 meetings, and in your team meetings. Pay close attention to their behavior and tone regarding the change. Stay curious, not judgmental.

Remember that a change announcement does not equal change communication. Prepare to discuss with each team member their reactions and their willingness to engage with the change.

1. List each team member's name.
2. Using your best guess, pick which zone each team member is in with the change.
3. Based on your observations, determine the reaction each person is having right now to the change: Move, Minimize, Wait, Resist, Quit/Quits. Remind yourself that this is a current snapshot, not a permanent reaction.
4. Consider how each team member is affected by or is affecting others in the change, then brainstorm reasons why each person might be reacting that way.
5. Using this assessment, schedule 1-on-1 meetings with each team member to discuss where they are with the change.

1. Name	2. Zone	3. Reaction	4. Thoughts on Why

During your 1-on-1, use any of these sample conversation starters:

- *My intent is to check in with you and listen to your experience of the recent change.*
- *What's been the impact of this change on you, your work, the team?*
- *I've noticed recently that you... [actual behaviors you've seen]. This leads me to believe you might be feeling less engaged. Tell me what you're feeling.*
- *What's challenging about the change for you? What concerns you most?*
- *Do you see any positives coming from the change? What are they?*
- *What opportunities do you see coming out of this change for you, the team, the organization?*

A Point of Decision During a Global Disruption

By the end of 2020, because of the COVID-19 pandemic, over 110,000 restaurants and bars in the US had closed: some temporarily, some permanently. That's 2.5 million jobs lost and a $240 billion drop in sales. And these weren't just startup restaurants struggling to get on their feet; most were well-established in the community, averaging sixteen years in business. Most large chains survived, but mom-and-pop establishments were hit hard.[25]

You remember what it was like. Most of us experienced gut-wrenching difficulties during the pandemic. Even if you weren't in the restaurant industry, dealing with the myriad of convergent disruptive forces they confronted, you almost certainly faced challenges and concerns related to getting food, whether from a grocery store or your favorite eating establishment. Many restaurants faced their own existential Point of Decision, including Four Foods Group.

Shauna Smith suddenly found herself and her company in the Zone of Disruption at the onset of the COVID-19 pandemic in March 2020. As the president of Four Foods Group, a company that owns and operates seventy-two restaurants, she saw a 40 percent, 50 percent, and, in some cases, 70 percent drop in revenue. Employees were scared to come to work, and customers were fearful about going to restaurants.

Like almost everyone on the planet, Smith and team were paralyzed at first—news releases, government mandates, and public sentiment seemed to shift constantly. It appeared that no matter what you did or didn't do, other people were going to disagree with your choices. Fear gripped the whole world.

Smith, a neighbor and friend of one of the authors, recounted her story. "There was an immediate fear...this unknown feeling," she said. "I didn't know what was going to happen or where we'd end up." But she understood that a leader's job is to remain calm in the face of such disruption and move forward. She told herself, "Okay... what I know is, I'm scared. That's okay. I recognize that. And I also know we've had challenges before, and cooler heads have always prevailed. So we'll stay cool and focus on the things we *can* control." Smith had reached her Point of Decision and had engaged with the change.

Recognizing what was within her control, Smith and her leadership team responded differently than many other restaurant operations at the time. Rather than just making it through the pandemic, they decided they were going to "thrive." To get the employees on board with such a vision, they recognized that what was needed was more clarity—something that, during a pandemic, was in short supply. She and her team scoured information sources to increase their understanding of what was going on so they could make informed decisions and paint a coherent picture of what the future would look like for their teams.

Smith said, "We would start at 6 a.m. We would gather in our war room every single morning for two to three hours and talk about any updates that were happening, like directives from the CDC or updates from our state health department.... As an executive team, we stayed in a constant state of communication."

They also increased dialogue with the employees to understand how they were reacting to the disruption and how they felt. They learned their teams were, understandably, confused about what to do. There was also a lot of fear; employees were asking, "Am I going to be able to pay my phone bill, and am I going to be able to pay my rent? Am I going to be able to put food on the table for my family?" And the questions kept coming: Would they still have a job? Would they get sick if they came to work? Would they risk bringing the sickness home to their loved ones? What was the company doing to protect employees?

Smith and her team committed to keep the doors open, to "just keep going…to keep showing up." They recognized the widespread fear, but also recognized that "when fear runs high, the need for courage runs higher." So they decided to "keep showing up for [their] team. [They] shifted into this purpose-driven mode with a mantra: 'stay safe, eat well, keep our teams working.'" They talked with their employees about safety: "We reassured our teams if they wanted to continue showing up, that we would have a job for them. But if they felt unsafe to come to work, that was okay. They could take a temporary leave of absence and when things settled down, they'd be welcomed back."

This was the key for many employees and helped ratchet down the fear. And even at this stage of the change, Smith and her team didn't know *how* they were going to address the difficulties ahead, but their optimism and empathy meant that many of their employees opted in to be a part of the solution. As a result, they "actually had very few people leave."

So, what were the solutions that Smith and company came up with? We'll discuss how they moved through the Zone of Adoption and Zone of Innovation in the upcoming chapters. For now, look at them as a model for how to move through the Zone of Disruption and get to the Point of Decision. They stayed calm during a global disruption, put their people first, and created dialogue to understand the impact of the change, then charted a path to the Point of Decision where employees could opt in (or out). And that is the goal of the Point of Decision: to move past the emotions of the change and take ownership over what to do next.

Asking, "What Now?"

"What now?" is the right question at the Point of Decision. It implies doing something different. The camaraderie born of going through a difficulty together can be a double-edged sword for your team: they can commiserate and complain and vent together… and stay stuck in the Zone of Disruption. Or they can come together with a determination to change their situation. Not everyone will be "all in"—there will likely be some more willing to own the change than others (remember *Move* in the parable?)—but fostering a general willingness to take on the responsibility of acting on the change will help pull the whole team along.

Leaders Clarify Rather Than Commiserate

Leaders must communicate that they, too, are engaged and an active participant in the change—with no hints of pessimism. Too often, change leaders feel like they should buddy up with those they lead and participate in the commiserating and complaining, even joining in the criticism of those who initiated the change. This only serves to keep the team stuck in the Zone of Disruption. Effective change leaders steer their team toward ownership of the problem by focusing on "What now?" With the Change Model framework as a guide, such leaders can orient their team to what lies ahead, not behind. They help their people understand that the Point of Decision is the decision to engage with the change, invest in the change, move toward the change, choose to be active and not passive, and do what needs to be done (not because someone is making them do it, but because they want to do it). They don't expect others to solve the problem for them. They make commitments and act. Ultimately, your team can come to recognize that, while they don't always get to choose whether a change happens to them, they do get to choose how they'll respond.

> *Ultimately, your team can come to recognize that, while they don't always get to choose whether a change happens to them, they do get to choose how they'll respond.*

Often a change is connected to a vision of where the company is trying to go or to a specific strategy. Remind people of that *why* as they make the commitment to join you on that journey.

Christi Phillips

Getting to Clarity Sooner (EMR Adoption, Part Four)

Whether it happens immediately or down the road, the refusal to own change will find its way back to you in an unpleasant way. It's easiest to own change early on, when it's relatively small. If you don't, it'll pick up steam and become more and more uncontrollable, until it's too much for you to handle.

As you've read previously, I was deep in the change trenches, helping a healthcare system implement updated technology. My colleagues and I realized some of the culture among mid-level managers may have been affecting the change protocols. As they saw it, executives had adopted a major plan with a very long timeline and huge budget, yet seemingly given little forethought to the way its implementation would affect frontline workers and the day-to-day business of patient care that still had to be managed along the way. Meanwhile, mid-level managers and those on the front lines of change had little visibility into the process, little influence on the outcome, and a murky picture of the project's overall direction or current status. There was a lot of top-down communication about future cost savings and other high-level administrative and strategic mumbo jumbo, but no connection to how nurses' work would change, how the finance team would have to learn to capture revenue differently, or who in IT was responsible for emergent technology problems related to the new system. While most people assumed leadership would provide clarity and training eventually, the further along the project got without these reassurances, the more uncomfortable and anxious everyone became.

This became a major hurdle for my team to overcome, and we had to find methods, big and small, to remedy the animosity between these two factions of the healthcare system. I remember one moment when the CEO had an opportunity to own the change, yet refused (to his eventual detriment). Rather than talking directly with his direct reports, he handed the conversation off to go-betweens in HR and other departments. Long experience has shown us that the most trusted change relationships involve the leader closest to you, and as you might expect, the least trusted involve those furthest from you in the organization—which generally means senior leadership. It's not because they're not trustworthy, but because you don't have the relationship. And that's what change leadership is about—the relationship between those going through the change and the ability to stay in open, honest, and productive dialogue throughout.

Not Everyone Arrives at the Point of Decision at the Same Time

Not all team members reach the Point of Decision at the same time, and not all team members make the same choice. They may:

* Choose to continue seeking clarity.

* Choose to disengage.
* Choose to engage.

As a leader, you can't decide for your team members, but you can influence the timing and direction of these choices.

Working With Those Who Choose to Continue Seeking Clarity

Imagine you are an administrator at a high school where each teacher in the building teaches an average of 150 students per day, sometimes across multiple subjects. The district rolls out a new curriculum and discipline program intended to produce better student behavior and improved state test scores. The staff preferred the old curriculum and handling discipline in their own unique ways. The new curriculum is unfamiliar and challenging and involves new technology that is not very intuitive.

Teacher morale drops along with students' grades. As a leader, these challenges are no surprise to you. It makes sense that getting used to the new curriculum, technology, and discipline approach will take some time (hopefully not too much time). It also makes sense to you that there will be some frustration (partly because this is the third change in curriculum in just five years!). You understand the change reactions, and you've seen them on display in faculty meetings, emails, and hallway discussions: *Wait, Minimize, Resist, Move, Quit,* and *Quits.* You anticipated there would likely be a decline in academic performance and that staff would have different reactions to the change. And you don't fault them for these things. It's how change works. But now it's time to turn the corner and head back to the slope of the change curve. It's time for you and the staff to make the choice to engage.

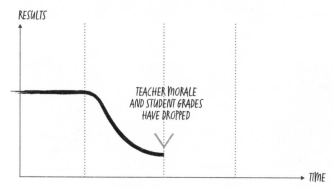

FIGURE 32: *Teachers at the Point of Decision.*

For some in the school, it can be tempting to think they don't have to make a choice, that they can delay or ignore the Point of Decision as they have many times before during their tenure in the district; that somehow things will go back to the way they were before; that students will grow and demonstrate greater proficiency; and that they can just exit the Zone of Disruption. But the Point of Decision is the door out of the Zone of Disruption. Those who avoid the door have still made a choice—they have chosen to stay in the zone longer.

Captain's Corner

Working With Those Who Need More Clarity

If you suspect people are dragging their feet because they lack the clarity they need to move to the Point of Decision, ask yourself:

- Who on my team hasn't reached the Point of Decision?
- What is holding them back?
- What is the cost to us because of their decision delay?
- What can I do to help them make their decision?

Then, in a 1-on-1, here's how you might conduct a conversation:

- I've noticed that [share facts regarding the minimizing, resisting, waiting, or quitting behaviors you've seen].
- This leads me to believe that you might need more clarity to help you get to the Point of Decision.

- How do you see it?
- What can we do to help you opt in and engage with the change?
- How can I help you choose to engage? What further clarification, background, or information do you need to make that decision?
- When should we check in again?

Working With Those Who Choose to Disengage or Leave

At the Point of Decision, your team members may choose to disengage—to not accept or engage in the change. This is essentially a choice to remain at lower results.

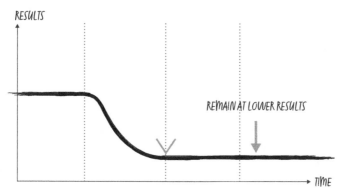

FIGURE 33: *Remain at Lower Results.*

As a leader, you may find that some of your people may not be happy about the change, and they choose to disengage. They drag their feet in quiet (or not-so-quiet) protest. Your role is to help them understand that, while a dip in results during the Zone of Disruption is understandable, continued poor results is not acceptable. The purpose of the change wasn't to produce worse results. Encourage them to choose to engage with the change instead of settling into a new and lower Zone of Status Quo.

Your team will need resilience and the ability to persist through difficulties and setbacks if they're going to be successful at change. In the parable, the captain reminded the crew that "Our charge is to take *Results* and her cargo to..." Even though they had experienced hardships, their goal and responsibilities remained the same. The crew had signed up for this. When they became crew members, they accepted the responsibility of taking the cargo to the destination.

Quit protests: "Well, the cargo can spoil for all I care. I hate it here."

To which the captain responds, "And we still have a job to do. That hasn't changed."

Help your team members understand that there will be changes, setbacks, and challenges on any difficult but meaningful journey toward a goal. They believed in that goal enough to sign on as a "crew member." And you, as their leader, believed in them then, as you still do now. That's why they're on your team. Help them remember why they signed on in the first place. But don't stop there. As you remind your team of the vision, the strategies to reach the vision, and their responsibilities, paint a picture of the opportunities they'll have access to if they opt in and walk through the Point of Decision and into the Zone of Adoption.

In *Who Rocked the Boat?*, it reads, "In the end, everyone had their own concerns and reactions, but what the crew mostly wanted was a clear, well-thought-out plan." That's understandable. People want the security of a "well-thought-out" plan. But that plan can only come when your team opens the door and chooses to engage. Remember, as much as people would like to see that plan before they engage (and as tempting as it is to just issue orders and get people moving), it's on the *other* side of the Point of Decision that the plan comes together and the real work begins.

Sometimes despite your best efforts, the Zone of Disruption may be too much for someone on your team. They may decide to quit and leave the organization. While this may feel to them (and other members of your team) like they've broken free from the Zone of Disruption, they're actually choosing a *different* change with its own Zone of Disruption and Point of Decision. Whether or not their change journey will lead to a better experience or greater opportunities for them, who knows? What is certain is that there will be change where they're going, and you would be well served to remind those "left behind" of this reality.

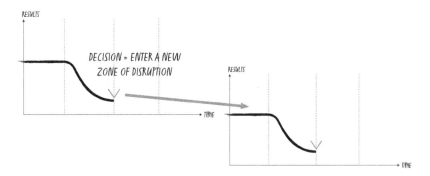

FIGURE 34: *Choosing a Different Change.*

As a leader, you have the challenge of working with the person threatening to jump ship. Losing people and rehiring is expensive. Keeping people who are disengaged is perhaps more expensive. It's a tough spot to be in for a leader. It's important for you, as a leader, to weigh the costs (not only in money and time, but also in team morale and culture) of helping someone stay; or waving and saying, "Good luck!" as they jump into the water and swim for shore.

Choosing the Change

At its core, coaching is all about change. It is about accessing support to change mindsets and behaviors to create different circumstances and to actualize aspirations and set goals. Whatever the details, clients rarely get into action or accomplish goals until they make the decision that they're up for change, whether suggested, imposed, or initiated. Otherwise, efforts to impact outcomes are delayed, and empowerment is often and unintentionally surrendered to others.

Marché Pleshette

The point is worth echoing: One thing that rarely works is a coaching or change agreement one does not agree to participate in. Years ago, a mother paid for her college-aged daughter to be coached by me. I knew from the first session she was not interested in the change her mother wanted. Neither the coaching nor the objective was ever her idea. Her mother had explained that the daughter was considering quitting school, which ran counter to a family value of higher education. The daughter wanted her own fulfilling life—not her mother's. Truthfully, that could have been a life-changing coaching goal, but she never reached a point of buy-in—neither for her goal, her mother's goal, nor the coaching itself. So while she had six sessions paid for and booked, she only attended two.

We never gain the momentum necessary for change until we cross the threshold of active participation via the Point of Decision. This is true for college students, executives, individual professionals, entrepreneurs, and free agents.

Now, contrary to the student's experience, there is such promise for someone who decides they're in! There is the example of a woman I coached who, after five years of being a director at her organization, set a goal of acquiring a more senior position. While it was her own decision to change, her plummet into the Zone of Disruption was no less disorienting. Disruption for her was the realization that her desire to be a senior leader at her organization was not necessarily shared by those in a position to promote her. Their perception of her value seemed to have been limited to her contribution as a mid-level manager. For the first time, she saw that a likely promotion would not be a given; it would not happen merely through the submission of a résumé.

She reflected on her situation and lamented that she had rarely been recognized for the level of proven accomplishments she'd already made as a leader. The change she wanted unveiled not only how others saw her, but even how she saw herself. It was daunting.

But then she had an epiphany. Either she would wait in vain for someone to make the advancement happen for her, or she would take responsibility for her professional advancements and success. She knew there were relationships to build, barriers to break, and a need to show up in a bigger way. Something clicked, and she chose to participate in the change she wanted. It's as if she said, "I am in control of my future. No one else is."

We never gain the momentum necessary for change until we cross the threshold of active participation.

And that was the Point of Decision that gave her the mojo (empowerment) to do whatever was necessary to become that senior leader she wanted to be! This is the place where every client and change agent believes it's possible to get a return on their investment of efforts, and it unleashes them to at least try!

Captain's Corner

Working With Those Who Choose to Disengage or Leave

How do you talk with those who are disengaged or thinking of jumping ship? In 1-on-1s, you might ask questions like these:

- I've noticed that you recently _____ [factual behaviors you've seen]. This leads me to believe you might feel less engaged at work or may be thinking of leaving the organization. Do you see it differently?
- Is something happening I might not be aware of that might help me better understand what's going on?
- How can I help you choose to stay and engage?
- We won't be in this disruption forever. We'll get out, move up the Zone of Adoption and then into the Zone of Innovation. How do you feel about opportunities that will come as we move through the change curve?

Gain Enough Commitment to Move to the Point of Decision

Of the options at the Point of Decision, only one opens the door to the possibilities offered in the Zones of Adoption and Innovation: choosing to engage with the change.

You and your team aren't guaranteed better results in the Zone of Adoption—you still have a lot of work ahead of you—but unlike the other choices, the way is open.

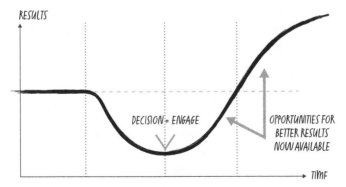

FIGURE 35: *Opening the Door to More Opportunities.*

Looking back at our education scenario, the leader's goal was to guide the teachers to the Point of Decision and help them reject the idea of settling into a lowered status quo. Such buy-in is more than a courtesy offered out of mere respect to the leader or their position. While it may be tempting to accept a deference to authority—lukewarm acceptance or *forced* compliance—and move your team into the next zone, ultimately you must judge when enough commitment is present to move through the Point of Decision. There is much more to be gained if you can invite your team to make the commitment and opt in for themselves.

Curtis Bateman

A Choice and a Changed Trajectory

As I referenced previously, in 2016, I moved to England with my wife and three kids. Upon arrival, my thirteen-year-old son, Calvin, started school. The stress of Calvin's new school and testing regime was compounded by the fact that he was suddenly in an all-boys school with uniforms: white shirts, blazers, black dress slacks, dress shoes, and a tie that matched the house colors.

It was obvious that Calvin hated it there, and the fact that I had imposed the change on him didn't help. The move to England was a radical departure from the way he was used to schooling—no girls, classes didn't change, and the grading system was vastly different. Plus, the tie!

For the first year, Calvin was stuck in the Zone of Disruption. Nothing was working. School and life felt miserable. Then after the first year, he realized there were choices he could make and things he could do. How did he come to this realization? As a dad and through my association with FranklinCovey and friendship with Sean Covey, who authored the bestselling teen leadership book *The 7 Habits of Highly Effective Teens*, I took a chance and handed my teenage son a copy of it. On reflection, I realize it took a year of struggles and frustrations for him to be at a point where a book like this could even make an impact. But it did. I like to think the counsel my wife and I gave him helped too. Regardless of the inputs, influences, and timing, moving through the Point of Decision was Calvin's decision to own. To our shared relief, he made it and never looked back.

Calvin began to figure out how school, his social life, and his job could all fit together. He decided to make it work—to manage what was within his control and not lament about what wasn't. As a result, he made choices that totally changed his trajectory over the remaining two years. He developed a group of friends and thrived academically. Calvin clarified how he came to see the change by reframing it into something he had some measure of control over. He was resilient enough to push through the uncertainty and newness of everything to find new opportunities on the other side. And it all began with him owning the change and his role in it. That was a decision only Calvin could make. And it certainly wasn't easy—that's the resilience part. But he found a new way forward.

Today Calvin looks back on the experience as something that has given him a broader world perspective and increased his capacity to move through the unexpected turns in life which is often the nature of change—disruptive, difficult, and confusing at first. If we learn to first endure and then take control of it, it can lead to new opportunities, levels of performance, and personal insights.

Team Members Can Influence Each Other Through the Point of Decision

In the above story, Calvin made his own decision to engage—it wasn't made by his parents. Likewise, in *Who Rocked the Boat?*, the captain didn't waste time barking orders through a megaphone. That wouldn't have gotten the crew to and through the Point of Decision. And while team members will have varying degrees of commitment and engagement, a team with enough momentum, enough consensus, and enough buy-in collectively can help and influence each other and make it through the Point of Decision together. In the parable, it reads, "The others nodded in agreement, although some less enthusiastically than others. But it was enough for *Wait* to see things were happening." *Wait* (and other crew members) felt the pull of their team as they reached a kind of decision tipping point. Sometimes that's all it takes.

As we mentioned earlier in the book, many leaders tell their people to just "embrace change," as if this phrase will magically get them past the Point of Decision.

A leader can guide someone to the Point of Decision door, but for change to succeed, each person will have to open and walk through it themselves.

It won't.

A leader can guide someone to the Point of Decision door, but for change to succeed, each person will have to open and walk through it themselves.

In the parable, the captain was gratified that the crew had decided to engage and enter the Zone of Adoption: "The captain was pleased they had decided to get to work, and knew getting out of the ravine would stretch the crew in ways they weren't used to."

As a leader, getting your people through that door is no small thing. But don't rest on those laurels too long; the real work is just about to begin.

Captain's Corner

Engage in Change Talk With Your Team

Even if, as a team, you've reached the Point of Decision and are moving into the Zone of Adoption, each team member may be more or less engaged. It's important to know their trajectory, because the next zone is where most changes fail.

- Assess where each team member is with the change, then write their initials in the boxes beneath the continuum below (and be sure to include your own):

AWAY  TOWARD

- Now plan a discussion, prioritizing those who are furthest "away." In your next 1-on-1:
  - **Ask and Listen**
    - What concerns you most about the change?
    - What clarity do you need?
    - What would success look like for you?
  - **Support**
    - What will help you feel more confident about the change?
    - How can the team or I support you in moving forward?

- **Plan**
  - What can we do to help you move "toward" the change—opting in and engaging with it?
  - When will we check in again?

From the Point of Decision to the Zone of Adoption

Moving through the Point of Decision requires personal buy-in and commitment. This is critical, as the momentum gained here will soon be put to the test in the Zone of Adoption.

CHAPTER EIGHT

The Zone of Adoption

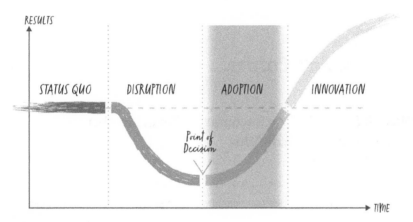

FIGURE 36: *The Zone of Adoption.*

Engage to Help Your Team Persist

The Zone of Adoption is where it's time for everyone to roll up their sleeves and begin a new type of work. This will come with its share of risk, as the Zone of Adoption is where most change efforts fail. As a leader, you must stay highly engaged throughout the climb to help your team persist through the trial-and-error nature of this zone.

Moving From "Problems" to "Obstacles to Overcome"

Leaders have a choice in how they view the Zone of Adoption. They can see it as a seemingly endless array of problems that will thwart their advance at every opportunity, or as a series of obstacles to overcome that will enable their team members to stretch themselves, learn, and grow as a result. We recommend the latter, as the challenges will come whether you embrace them or not. But how such a crucible strengthens (or breaks) your team will be largely up to you. The Zone of Adoption requires new approaches to new challenges, which means a good deal of trial and error to figure things out. The most effective change leaders make it safe for their team to learn from the resulting failures, strengthening rather than weakening their "change muscle" as they continue the ascent.

 Captain's Corner

Make It Safe to Fail by Encouraging Team Members to Surface Obstacles With You

With your individual team members, in 1-on-1s or in team meetings, use these questions to identify, understand, and sort obstacles to change using three categories: hurdles (obstacles team members can handle on their own); quicksand (obstacles that require others' help); and brick walls (obstacles that need to be passed to the leader to solve). Brainstorm with them possible solutions to overcome each.

At the end of the meeting, thank the team member for having the courage to share the obstacles and ask for help. Express the confidence you have in them to overcome the obstacle and achieve change success.

OBSTACLE	POSSIBLE SOLUTION
What hurdles do you face that you can overcome on your own?	What is your mindset relative to this change?
	What have you tried so far?
	What possible solutions might fix the problem?
	What might you need to stop doing to prioritize and address this obstacle?

What quicksand is slowing you down or causing you to get stuck?	In what ways are you struggling on your own that might be getting you more stuck?
	Who or what might help you out of the quicksand?
	What other possible solutions should we consider?
	What might we need to stop doing to prioritize and address this obstacle?
What brick walls have you hit that you need to pass along to me to fix? (The purpose of this category is to capture everything that hasn't been sorted into hurdles or quicksand. The goal of the leader is to find a last appropriate category for everything that's left.)	What's left?
	Am I the right person?

Reactions in the Zone of Adoption

Gathered on the beach, hemmed in by the steep walls and jungle, the crew in *Who Rocked the Boat?* came together to brainstorm a plan for getting up the cliff: deconstructing the ship, then building a series of ladders, platforms, and pulleys. In the Zone of Adoption, leaders are often called on to deconstruct the tools, processes, systems, models, or structures that *used* to work prior to the change. This means the crew faced a great deal of difficulty and trial-and-error problem solving during their ascent:

> But even Minimize *had underestimated the required effort. It was extremely hard work. They had to find a suitable spot on the rock wall, hold the ladder in place, climb, secure it, build a small platform, then hand the next ladder up, repeating the process over and over. Sometimes the crew came to spots where they couldn't find any good places to fasten the ladder and had to back down and try a different route. Sometimes they had to lay the ladder sideways and travel in a direction they didn't want to go, hoping to find another way up. Other times, the wind threatened to blow them off the cliff! These and many more challenges had to be overcome as the crew zigzagged across the cliff's face, sometimes*

moving up, sometimes moving sideways, and sometimes moving down; but eventually and persistently, they continued the ascent.

In the Change Model, our line that moves steadily up and to the right (which is a useful abstraction for a model) looks more chaotic in real life:

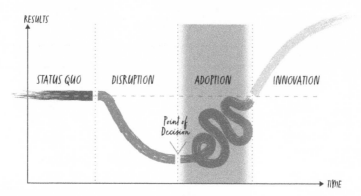

FIGURE 37: *The Squiggly Line.*

Notice how the different reactions of the crew in the face of a major setback play out in the Zone of Adoption:

> *It turned out, much to their dismay, that* Quit *had been right all along. The parts were too heavy, even with all their pulleys and the mast for support! Try as they might, the crew just couldn't muster enough strength to pull the heavy bundles up.*

From *Quit* celebrating a predicted failure, *Wait* watching from the sidelines, *Minimize* lamenting what was supposed to work but didn't, and *Move* wanting to celebrate what they *had* accomplished, to *Resist* using sarcasm to make a point, this is a crew in need of engagement! Which is exactly what the captain does:

> *"Move does have a point," the captain said, knowing just how hard the crew had worked to get to where they were. "We solved all kinds of challenges on the cliff."*
>
> *As the crew reflected on how hard they had worked, it did feel as if they had become better at figuring out how to overcome the unexpected.*

Despite the failures that naturally occur in the Zone of Adoption, those going through it are building change muscle if they persist. Which is what's happening for the crew. But it requires the captain to stay engaged, offering encouragement and support when needed:

> *Realizing all they had accomplished and with the captain's encouragement to try again, the crew shifted from complaining to solving the problem in front of them.*

Much like the Point of Decision in the larger change journey, the crew must reengage with the change and recommit—perhaps several times—during the Zone of Adoption. This is the nature of the climb. For our crew, they eventually repurpose the boilers into a steam-powered winch. That level of problem solving will pay additional dividends in the Zone of Innovation, but for now, it's enough to get the captain and crew out of the dip and back to the River Routine.

Without the ongoing and effective engagement of the captain throughout the Zone of Adoption, the crew would have never made it up the cliff (or for that matter, even attempted the ascent). By contrast, the shortcomings of a disengaged or command-and-control leader will be laid bare—there are no shortcuts in the Zone of Adoption.

The shortcomings of a disengaged or command-and-control leader will be laid bare—there are no shortcuts in the Zone of Adoption.

Shauna Smith and Four Foods Group

In our case study from Chapter Seven, Shauna Smith and her leadership team had successfully led their employees to the Point of Decision. Now it was time for the Zone of Adoption ascent. With their mantra and vision of "stay safe, eat well, keep our teams working," Smith, the leadership team, and the employees jumped in with both feet. They had obstacles to overcome for their employees, customers, and the broader community, in that order. But how? They didn't have all the answers, but they worked hard to figure things out as they went along—a hallmark of being in the Zone of Adoption.

Smith said, "We immediately focused on the 'stay safe' part of our mantra. That meant being deliberate about things like wearing face masks and how we set up our cleaning schedules."

Did everything they tried work? Not at all—there were setbacks. "The mistakes came. There were things we tried and threw out...we realized something that we thought was going to work didn't. And that was a constant along the way."

But Smith and her team stayed engaged, persevered, and made it safe for their employees to try new things. They experimented with cleaning schedules, cleaning supplies, and systems of communication. They worked together, brainstorming and trying new things. Again, some worked, others didn't. But they learned from what didn't work and kept going. And they began to see success. As Smith recalled, "Employees said to us that they felt safer at work than they did in their own homes."

Another factor in addressing employees' insecurities was that many of her employees couldn't get essentials like milk, eggs, and toilet paper. So the leadership team started providing meals for their employees and families. "We bought meat, milk, and eggs for all our team members. And then we said, every time you come to work, we'll give you a family pack. We would give them a full meal for six people."

Now it was time to turn their attention to their customers. How were they going to work through the Zone of Adoption to figure out how to serve their patrons? Smith said, "Once the employees were taken care of, we shifted our focus to the customer. That was where we stood up newly crafted pick-up stations. We had all our employees masked up and wearing personal protective equipment, and that made our customers feel better...they didn't even have to get out of their cars. They could place orders online."

Putting safeguards in place was important, but customers needed to understand how things now worked at the restaurants. "I'm pretty sure nobody figured out immediately that signage was going to be important. We were telling the customers what we were doing...we were keeping our trust with them," Smith reported. "We had QR codes. You could pull up pretty much to any one of our restaurants and know what to do because of all of the signage."

Another challenge that surfaced during the Zone of Adoption was knowing when to reopen restaurant lobbies. Smith recalled, "Some of the mistakes came with just not knowing how fast to move or how slow to move when it came to reopening lobbies. In some locations, I know we waited too long to open the lobbies back up. I think we had lost a bit of our customers' trust at first…but eventually we opened the doors. And finally, they returned."

Their climb through the trial-and-error nature of the Zone of Adoption continued. "It was absolute acrobatics to keep our teams working and to keep our customers eating. That was what we did. And we learned to be agile, that's for sure. We were gymnasts," Smith recounted. "And then there were the supply chains…don't even get me started! Where do we get cups? Where do we get straws? Where do we get syrup? We saw increases in protein prices, paying double and triple on our beef prices. It was a daily battle for all the different supplies that we needed for our brands, but we learned what not to do. That's the thing it taught us: to be as prepared as we can and have a plan so that we knew how we're going to react."

As a result of the supply-chain problems and other difficulties, Smith and her team changed their menu. Some changes worked, and customers didn't seem to mind. One change didn't go over well, however. "We took nachos off the menu (because they were labor-intensive and exposed the food to more hands that people thought might harbor the virus). And I cannot tell you how many of our customers were mad at us for it…we went back to the drawing board and recreated the nachos so that they were not only more efficient, but more delicious as well."

The leaders at Four Foods Group were feeling the effects of being on the squiggly line of change. Yet, they stayed engaged and persisted. "I would be in the stores, and I would hear good ideas from the hourly employees, from our management team there at the front of the line. They have the best ideas. And so that's where for me, I love that I don't have to be the creator of all the best ideas—it can come from all around me. I just have to be really good at listening and saying, 'That's the one. Let's run with that.'"

By coming up with these solutions, Smith and her team were able to climb

> *I would hear good ideas from the hourly employees, from our management team there at the front of the line. They have the best ideas…I just have to be really good at listening.*

through the Zone of Adoption. Their status quo had been employees who felt comfortable coming to work, customers who came into their stores, and brands that ran efficiently. Then the pandemic disruption threw everything out the window. The Zone of Adoption was difficult—it was a grind, but by staying engaged and making it safe to try new things, they found their way back to a "new normal." And through that, they had learned and changed as well. But the story's not over yet. In the next chapter, we'll show you how they took their newly formed change muscle and momentum and used them as springboards for innovation.

Adopting Through the Change

Think of the word *adopt*. When you *adopt* a course of action, you follow that course. The dictionary uses phrases such as "to take up and practice or use," "to accept," "to take by choice," and "to become the owner or caretaker of." To *adopt* is to own or take responsibility for something. The Zone of Adoption is where you take responsibility for the change. Leaders often believe that, once they've made the decision to engage, they can just jump straight to innovation and new outcomes. They don't realize they have to prime the pump of creativity, that they must try new things. They don't realize the need to *adopt* the change, or "take up and practice" the change, or "become the owner and caretaker" of the change. As a leader, give your people the freedom to figure out how to navigate the difficulties of the Zone of Adoption. "Ah, yes, innovation," you may think. "We're an innovative company. We give our people the freedom to innovate." Great, but not yet, as you haven't reached the optimal point to innovate. The Zone of Adoption and the Zone of Innovation are different, and it's vital that leaders understand the difference. We're not saying zero innovation happens in the Zone of Adoption, but that the best time to innovate in a way connected to the change is in the Zone of Innovation (as we'll explain in the next chapter). In the Zone of Adoption, you lay the groundwork for innovation to take place.

Engaging Your Team

There are different types of engagement, and change leaders recognize that the challenges in the Zone of Adoption often require the discretionary effort of all involved—not simply compliance, or just cooperation, but excitement.

FIGURE 38: *Types of Engagement.*

Too often, leaders are satisfied with compliance. But in the Zone of Adoption, compliance is unlikely to promote the kind of discretionary effort necessary to move through the trial-and-error nature of the climb. The difference between compliance and cooperation is the choice to opt in and take ownership of the individual's role in the change. Leaders with team members who fall into this category should revisit the Point of Decision Captain's Corners and help guide team members to make (or remake) the decision to engage with the change. However, they are unlikely to do so if they don't feel they are a valued member of the team. As a leader, this means listening to them, validating their struggles, and soliciting their ideas.

Team members who are actively cooperating likely represent the majority of those going through the Zone of Adoption. After all, not everyone can marshal the continued enthusiasm of *Move*, especially when they're in the midst of an uphill climb! Because cooperation is a team-driven activity, it's essential that leaders help members feel they are a part of a *winning* team, even in the face of setbacks. This is accomplished by celebrating the small wins along the way and recognizing their persistent effort in the face of adversity.

The highest level of engagement is labeled "excitement," which is an emotional outcome of being fully committed to the change. Leaders working to move their team members from cooperation to excitement focus on values—specifically, connecting the dots between what the team member values and the successful implementation of the change. Or said another way, the team member feels they are engaged in *meaningful* work—they see what they're doing as their contribution to the desired future vision. The foundation for this began in the Zone of Status Quo, and it's here, in the Zone of Adoption, that that investment pays off. The effective change leader reconnects the work the team is doing to the vision already shared and bought in to, rather than laying out the vision for the first time in the middle of the ascent, and hoping it will be motivating enough. For a leader, this also requires you to be seen as highly competent and having high character. After all, commitment (and the excitement that follows) can't happen without trust between the leader and their team. If trust is lacking, a future vision, no matter how eloquently articulated, will likely be met with skepticism and doubt.

Captain's Corner

Increase Your Team's Level of Engagement

Consider the three levels of engagement and "map" where your team members are. (It is likely that most members of the team will fall into the "cooperate" level of engagement, thus the bell-shaped curve).

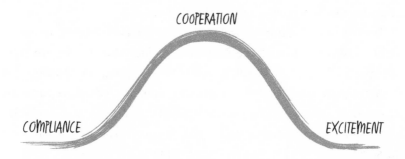

COOPERATION

COMPLIANCE

EXCITEMENT

In the space above, write the initial of each team member and where you believe they fall. Then do the following:

- For team members at the "compliance" level of engagement:
  - Revisit the Captain's Corners in the "Point of Decision" chapter and schedule a time to go through one with your team member.
  - Make sure you've communicated that they are a valued member of the team, by:
    - Actively listening to them.

- ◆ Validating their struggles, worries, or concerns.
- ◆ Soliciting their ideas for how to make things better.
- To help team members get to and/or not slip from the "cooperation" level of engagement:
  - Help them feel they are part of a winning team, even in the face of setbacks and failures.
  - Make it safe to try, fail, learn, and try again.
  - Take time to celebrate small wins.
  - Validate and recognize their struggle in the face of adversity.
  - Acknowledge the obstacles to be overcome and prioritize and/or minimize them the best you can.
- To help team members get to and/or not slip from the "excitement' level of engagement:
  - Connect that team member's value to the successful implementation of the change.
  - Help them see they are engaged in meaningful work by showing them how their contributions further the realization of the bigger picture and vision.
  - Make sure you are seen as highly competent and having high character through what you do and how you treat others. (In our *Leading at the Speed of Trust* practice, we teach these high-trust behaviors as Demonstrate Respect, Listen First, Practice Accountability, Confront Reality, Talk Straight, and Extend Trust.)

Resourcefulness and the Story of Change

The Zone of Adoption requires resourcefulness. You see this in great stories, books, and movies—they're all about change. In fact, most movies parallel the Change Model:

Zone of Status Quo

- ◆ *Harry Potter and the Sorcerer's Stone:* Harry Potter lives in the cupboard under the stairs.
- ◆ *The Lord of the Rings:* Frodo Baggins lives comfortably in the Shire.

- *Moana:* Moana lives peacefully and prosperously on the island Motunui as the chief's daughter.

Zone of Disruption

- *Harry Potter and the Sorcerer's Stone:* Harry learns about his parents' death at the hands of Lord Voldemort and begins a new life at Hogwarts.
- *The Lord of the Rings:* Frodo must flee the Shire and begin a quest to destroy the Ring.
- *Moana:* Motunui's food sources are threatened by a supernatural plague and Moana must find a solution.

Point of Decision

- *Harry Potter and the Sorcerer's Stone:* Harry and his friends decide to get the Sorcerer's Stone before Snape does.
- *The Lord of the Rings:* Frodo decides to separate from the Fellowship and make the journey into Mordor with Sam.
- *Moana:* Moana must venture off the island to find the demigod Maui, who will help her restore the heart of Te Fiti, despite the wrathful Te Ka blocking their way.

Zone of Adoption

- *Harry Potter and the Sorcerer's Stone:* Harry and his friends overcome the obstacles set up to protect the Sorcerer's Stone.
- *The Lord of the Rings:* Frodo and Sam overcome the various threats and obstacles along the perilous journey to Mordor.
- *Moana:* Moana learns wayfinding from Maui, and they overcome obstacles like the Kakamora and the giant crab Tamatoa in the Realm of Monsters.

Zone of Innovation

- *Harry Potter and the Sorcerer's Stone:* Harry defeats Professor Quirrell through a powerful counter-charm placed on him by his mother.
- *The Lord of the Rings:* Frodo loses his battle with Gollum but gains new

insight into the self-diminishing nature of evil and the power of mercy.

♦ *Moana:* Moana restores the heart of Te Fiti when she makes peace with Te Ka, restoring balance and prosperity to her home island of Motunui.

In the examples above, the heroes learn something about themselves that they didn't know before and would not have learned had they not gone through the trials of change. They had to stretch themselves—no epic journey is easy. Resourcefulness and persistence are key. Perhaps the reason we continue to tell such stories about change is because life *is* change, and the Zone of Adoption is where hard lessons are learned, valuable skills are honed, and new personal insights are gained. As a change leader, you are the author of the story of change for yourself and your team—not always regarding the outside events that spurred it, but how, like the heroes in the stories we know hold true over time, you and your team will use those challenges to change and grow. This is especially true in the Zone of Adoption.

> *As a change leader, you are the author of the story of change for your team.*

Marché Pleshette

Persist Through Setbacks

To illustrate the experience within the Zone of Adoption, I'd like to continue with the story I shared about the coaching client who was seeking a senior leader position. Having reached the Point of Decision was pivotal, but it was only the threshold into a space where she would try doing whatever it took to accomplish her goal. The strategies and efforts to make it happen were the real work, and she entered the Zone of Adoption determined to succeed.

She'd had her eye on and pursued a particular position, and she got to a second interview for it, but not an offer. After applying for another position and going through a second round of interviews, she considered how her lack of assertion and her "fading presence" in her day-to-day exchanges might have been contributing to the missed opportunities. She was brilliant, but she did not show up as self-assured, so there was work to do on confidence.

In one of her sessions, she mentioned how she was often talked over in meetings, and how demeaning and self-betraying it felt to never have addressed it. So she worked on courage. She decided that the next time it happened, she would have a conversation with whomever might so easily disregard her. It happened again, and she addressed it. And... it did not go well. The colleague trivialized her concern and demeaned her. Although that was one person's perspective, it was crushing. The ups and downs of the efforts she was making on her change journey were at times enough to cause her to reevaluate her commitment to the change.

She began to feel her energy atrophy whenever she walked into the building for work. How could she possibly be seen as a leader when her disposition mirrored self-doubt? So at that point, she worked on both her body language and self-confidence. She straightened her posture, and she strategically took on projects and presentations that she hadn't before; she was determined to make more eye contact and was generally more intentional in showing up as the leader she aimed to be.

She made other efforts and purposely communicated with other leaders during and after meetings. Some things were more rewarding than others. We coached through discouraging days and celebrated and leveraged the successful ones. She never achieved a senior leadership role in her organization, but about six months after our coaching engagement, she obtained a position with greater influence at an even better company. I received a message from her over a year ago that said, "I wanted you to know that I received another promotion. Two promotions in three years. Thanks for your guidance and support. I carry it with me daily." Talk about the reward of change!

The Zone of Adoption might be a squiggly line, but with persistence, it transports us eventually to accomplishing the change goal and helps us to become masters of change.

 # Captain's Corner

Talking Through the Squiggly Line in the Zone of Adoption

As much we'd all like the Zone of Adoption to be a smooth ride up and to the right, it's a challenging zigzag up the side of the cliff. In 1-on-1s or with your team, consider asking the following questions:

- Which of the reactions describes you when navigating the squiggly line in the Zone of Adoption? (Wait, Move, Resist, Minimize, Quit, other?) Why?

- How comfortable are you with ambiguity? If you're not comfortable, what do you do to manage anxiety/stress?
- How does that reaction help or hinder the necessary problem solving in this zone?
- What has our team learned from the things that didn't work?
- As we try new approaches, how will we determine if we're moving sidewise, down, or up?

Making It Safe to Try New Things

Imagine you've been asked to step in last-minute as the director of a community play. One night, during the first act, an important piece of the set topples over and breaks. The set piece is vital to the story as scripted, and now it's unusable. But between acts, you invite your talented actors to just roll with the change and give them permission to improvise. They do so, adopting a new approach to the next scene without skipping a beat. The audience loves it. They saw what happened and were impressed by how well the actors improvised.

Alternatively, instead of inviting the actors to try something new, as the director, you could have walked on stage, grabbed the mic, and announced: "I'm sorry, but this isn't how the play is supposed to go. Someone's sloppy work has ruined the production, and we can no longer follow the script as written. There's nothing left to do, so the play has been canceled. Also, no refunds." You'd probably get booed off the stage, if not incite a riot!

Obviously, we've taken some creative license here. (Are you really the best candidate to direct a community-theater production? Maybe you are… no judgment here.) Unfortunately, in the Zone of Adoption, many leaders don't give their people the space to figure things out; they don't give them permission to try new things. Such leaders expect their team members to "stick with the script" as written. Sometimes leaders explicitly forbid their teams to take any creative license. In her book *Multipliers: How the Best Leaders Make Everyone Smarter,* author Liz Wiseman writes about the difference between Tyrants and Liberators. "Tyrants create a *tense* environment that suppresses people's thinking and capability. As a result, people hold back, bring up safe ideas that the leader agrees with, and work cautiously. Liberators create an intense environment that requires people's best thinking and work. As a result, people offer their best and boldest thinking and give their best effort."[26]

The Zone of Adoption is rarely, if ever, a predictable process that unfolds as planned and follows "the script." Successful change leaders make it safe for their teams to be bold and to try, and even improvise, new things.

Communicate the Strategy and Delegate the Tactical

Some countries in Europe are going through a massive change—digitalization—as companies try to figure out how to adopt digital technologies into the way they do business. Siemens is one such company working on this. In the past, Siemens's focus was mostly on manufacturing. They built trains, healthcare equipment, wind turbines, and many other large industrial products. With digitalization, they are now expanding their offerings to also include technology services, such as monitoring data on the trains so they can help their customers get the most out of their equipment and know when maintenance might be needed.[27] Good changes, important changes, but what does this change mean for the employees? They're now in the Zone of Adoption.

> *Leaders are most effective when they continue to communicate the strategy but let those closest to the work manage the tactical.*

In the Zone of Adoption, leaders are most effective when they continue to communicate the strategy but let those closest to the work manage the activities that support the strategy. Trust your people. They'll figure it out as you stay engaged and ensure alignment. In the case of Siemens, they sent a powerful message of trust to their people. "The coronavirus crisis has triggered a surge in digitalization.... These changes will also be associated with a different leadership style, one that focuses on outcomes...," explained Roland Busch, Deputy CEO and Labor Director of Siemens AG. "We trust our employees and empower them to shape their work themselves so that they can achieve the best possible results."[28]

As a leader, are you allowing your team members to "shape" their work in the Zone of Adoption, or insisting they follow the script as previously written?

Captain's Corner

Gaining Clarity on Trying New Things

Permission to try new things is important, but is it "anything goes"? What does permission look like in your organization or on your team? As a team, consider discussing the following:

- What does permission to try new things look like?
    - Is it a blanket permission?
    - Is it assumed our roles come with that permission?
    - Does someone grant permission specific to each thing we try?
- If we have someone give specific permissions, how does that person not become a bottleneck?
- We don't have unlimited time and budget to travel the squiggly line. How can we try things (knowing some won't work) without breaking the bank?
- We still have our "day jobs." How do we continue to fulfill our responsibilities while we figure things out?
- What's the right level of initiative we can take based on our current capabilities and the risks associated with this change? (Consider using the diagram below to help create a common language for levels of initiation and self-empowerment.)

LEVELS OF INITIATIVE/SELF-EMPOWERMENT

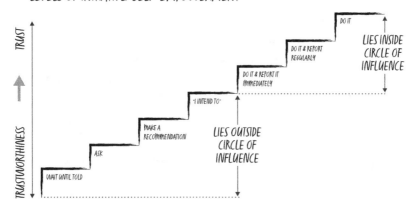

Finding the Win With Limited Resources

Resourceful people put available resources to efficient or ingenious use. The key word here is "available." What do your people have access to? Often budgets are tight, and teams must make do with what they have. As a leader, don't ask the *impossible*, but don't shy away from the *difficult*. Constraints and a lack of resources can create focus and foster creativity.

> **As a leader, don't ask the impossible, but don't shy away from the difficult.**

Consider the popular TV show *Chopped*, where the contestants must use four mystery ingredients to make food that is both delicious and impressive in presentation. The chefs have a mere thirty minutes to formulate a plan, cook, and plate everything, using all the basket ingredients. Talk about constraints! Yet, they often come up with amazing creations. Not *despite* the intense constraints, but *because* of them. Inviting your team to see constraints not as a limitation but a creative challenge can help them stay engaged and persist through the difficulties of the Zone of Adoption.

 ## Captain's Corner

Evaluate What Stays and What Goes

During adoption of a change, people can feel overwhelmed and frustrated by the perceived lack of progress. Not only are they expected to do their regular jobs, but they're also asked to take on brand-new actions to succeed in the change.

Do the following activity with your team to evaluate current work tasks and processes, and decide what to stop doing to increase energy and focus for the change. The goal is to identify two to four things your team can stop doing to increase change capacity.

- Record the team's consistent tasks and routines (not just change-related ones).
- For each one, ask, "What happens if we stop doing this?" (Consider the

wider impact on other teams, departments, stakeholders, customers, etc.)

- Identify who needs to validate or authorize your ideas.
- Get the ideas validated.

WHAT IS THE TASK/ ROUTINE?	WHAT HAPPENS IF WE STOP DOING IT?	SHOULD IT STAY?	SHOULD IT GO?

Christi Phillips

Minimizing Losses as a Small Win (EMR Adoption, Part Five)

The Zone of Adoption is all about navigating the challenges associated with attempting something new once you've decided to act. It's about increasing your awareness, testing new truths, and developing understanding. It's a difficult and often awkward growth phase in which you can end up in a better state than you were at the beginning of the zone.

In the midst of the massive EMR change I was going through, even seasoned change agents didn't know how difficult the adoption would be. There were technology problems, financial albatrosses, and leadership potholes that didn't show up until we were right up on them! While a timeline for implementation can try to account for delays and thoughtful financial planning can keep creditors at bay, we cannot know the magnitude of some of the other problems, and they can be overwhelming. We can seem so far away from a solution—a win—that we may get discouraged and may want to give up. We need wins to keep going. You've heard that celebrating small wins is important. I've also learned that minimizing losses can be a small win that encourages you onward toward your goal.

For example, one medical organization I worked with was losing $2 million per quarter in billing. The big win goal was to keep from losing any money and to bring in $1 million per quarter. But reaching that goal was a huge, daunting task. Very discouraging. Rather than focusing on the goal of making $1 million per quarter, we found it was much more encouraging to celebrate losing less. If we lost $2 million last quarter, and only lost $1 million this quarter, that's a win! We were moving in the right direction. We celebrated that win to maintain the momentum toward the eventual big win of making money. Minimizing losses and celebrating those wins can be a valuable precursor for big wins.

We continued to take pride in the little victories ("This quarter we only lost $500,000!"). As time went on, we stopped minimizing losses and started to post victories again. After all the growing pains and reconfiguring, the healthcare teams and systems came out better than before. The change wasn't easy, but it was worth it.

Change leaders have the power (and responsibility) to define what winning means. This matters, especially when constraints make the change even more daunting. But finding and celebrating little victories along the way is all part of the squiggly-line journey of the Zone of Adoption. And over time, those little victories can aggregate into a larger organizational win.

Captain's Corner

Fostering Creativity in Constraints

When you ask people to be resourceful and look at constraints as a creative opportunity, what do you mean exactly? To help make this idea actionable, consider asking:

- What resources do you already have to solve the challenge ahead?
- Rather than focusing on what's missing, how might these resources be used in new ways?

- Knowing that some things we try won't work, how do we minimize the costs of failure without stifling creativity?

Helping Team Members Recommit When Stalled

As we highlighted earlier, as many as 70 percent of change initiatives fail to reach their desired objectives. And the Zone of Adoption is where the failure is most likely to happen.

But it doesn't have to be that way.

As a leader, help your people maintain their resolve. People often don't feel prepared for, or empowered to handle, the "now whats" that come with subsequent challenges. Therefore, it's important for leaders to understand and empathize with the discouragement, disorientation, and frustration that appear in this zone. Even the resolve engendered at the Point of Decision can wane under the pressure of the ascent. Your team members may question their ability to handle the changes. They may not have trust that their teammates can pull it off, nor trust you as a leader, thinking you're setting them up for failure. This can occur because they question your relevance or your track record.

The obstacles in the Zone of Adoption are real. Acknowledge those obstacles. Label them and face them with the help of the obstacles tool introduced earlier. Minimize them by allowing your people to solve what they can on their own and clearing the roadblocks when they can't. Persist. Keep going. Grit is required in this zone. But the payoff extends beyond just getting back to the Zone of Status Quo. Your team, under your careful guidance, can be set up to do even more than before. That's the true promise of change.

Captain's Corner

Helping Your Team Members Recommit

If someone on your team has lost their resolve, talk with them. It may be a matter of their mindset, confidence, or trust. In a 1-on-1 with this person, you might ask:

- You seemed like you accepted responsibility for the change and were engaged before. What happened?
- At this point in our change journey, do you feel like you're more like Move, Minimize, Wait, Resist, or Quit?
- How is your current reaction impacting results?
- What makes you believe we can/can't pull this off?
- Is there something specific about how we're implementing the change that you don't have confidence in? Are you comfortable sharing this?
- What would restore your faith and trust?

From the Zone of Adoption to the Zone of Innovation

Moving out of the Zone of Adoption is a huge accomplishment. With that success come newly formed change muscles and problem-solving skills ready to be put to further use in the Zone of Innovation.

CHAPTER NINE

The Zone of Innovation

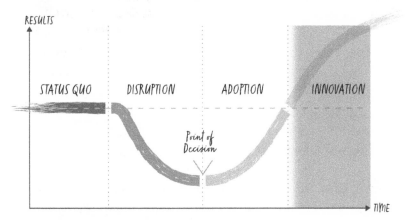

FIGURE 39: *The Zone of Innovation.*

Change and the Nature of Innovation

One of the themes of this book is how to maximize the amount of return on investment (ROI) for a given change. Because the Zone of Adoption naturally requires a degree of creativity, leaders and their teams will realize things they didn't know at the beginning of the change. The Zone of Innovation invites teams to do something with the Zone of Adoption discoveries and create even more benefit from their change work. The Zone of Innovation is an invitation to extend the existing change curve "up and to the right," rather than enacting an entirely new change initiative and resetting to the Zone of Disruption (although this may occur organically, it is not the leadership aim of this zone).

Consider the sport of rugby, where the objective is for two teams to "run past, through, and over their opponents in an effort to ground the ball inside the in-goal area...."[29] Similar to American football, one metric for success is "yards after contact," or how far the ball-carrier can continue pushing forward after making contact with a defender. This concept works for the Zone of Innovation as well—the strategy is not to give up and lie down after you get hit, but to leverage the newly acquired change muscle to carry your momentum and move the ball even farther down the field.

THE LEADERSHIP FOCUS IN THE ZONE OF INNOVATION *IS* ABOUT...	THE LEADERSHIP FOCUS IN THE ZONE OF INNOVATION *IS NOT* ABOUT...
• Connecting to the current change initiative. • Extending the change curve further up and to the right. • Leveraging the team's newly acquired change muscle and momentum. • Inviting a sense of directed curiosity.	• Creating an entirely new change initiative. • Resetting the process to the Zone of Disruption. • Engaging in blue sky ideation decoupled from the current change. • Incubating prototypes.

Keep in mind, we're not suggesting that anything in the right column is bad. It's just that leaders in the Zone of Innovation have a specific opportunity and, depending upon their role, responsibility. The nature of the organization or industry they're in and the desired and acceptable scope of innovation can vary wildly—but *not* when innovation is connected to the change itself, which is where the Zone of Innovation really shines. Consider how this played out at the turn of the twentieth century, when businesses were faced with an unprecedented change.

Ice harvesting had been a long-standing part of human history. The cutting and storing of ice to preserve food began in China near 1000 BCE. Five hundred years later, Egyptians and Indians began making their own by filling shallow earthenware pots with water and setting them out on cold nights. During the eighteenth century, farmers sold ice from their ponds, mostly purchased by the wealthy, who could afford ice houses.

In the nineteenth century, the demand for ice steadily increased, and the technology for harvesting it improved. The horse-pulled ice plow was invented in 1825 and ice trade became a global affair. Blocks of natural ice were exported from the United States to destinations as far as Rio de Janeiro,

Sydney, and Calcutta. This network of ice shipping allowed other exports, such as fish, butter, and eggs, to travel alongside the frozen cargo. By 1850, demand for ice in the United States grew so high that 2 million tons of it were being stored in warehouses. And that number only increased as a wave of immigrants to New York, Baltimore, and Philadelphia drove demand even higher.

Through the first part of the twentieth century, Americans grew more accustomed to the benefits of having access to a ready supply of ice. They could enjoy and keep milk, fresh meat, fruit, seafood, and produce, as nearly every family, grocer, and barkeeper owned an ice box. New apartment buildings were built with ice doors that opened into the kitchen.

Then came the electric residential refrigerator in 1913. At first, only the wealthy could afford them, but as the price came down, sales took off. The more people bought electric refrigerators, the less they demanded ice deliveries, which meant the companies that provided such services were seeing their market quickly decline. This created a massive disruption and sent those in the ice-delivery business into the Zone of Disruption.

John Jefferson Green was one of those disrupted by the change. He worked for the Southland Ice Company in Dallas, and he and his company had to face the fact that their ice-delivery sales were dropping off. They worked their way through the Zone of Adoption and became a refrigeration company. Having arrived at the Zone of Innovation, Green could have called it done and accepted the new status quo. But instead, he wondered what else he could do. After all, he still had all his former ice warehouses scattered throughout the city and in close proximity to his customers. And they had plenty of refrigeration units. Why not fill those refrigerators with staples and make it convenient for customers to buy cold items like eggs and milk? Green and his company moved through the "big" change—from ice to refrigeration. They were at liberty to explore what else that big change could lead to. As a result, you've likely seen their "convenience" stores yourself, now with over 70,000 locations in seventeen countries.[30] This change innovation—not pivoting to the new technology, but using their refrigerators and locations to imagine and do something more—became the genesis for 7-Eleven, now known the world over.

Had the disruption of electric household refrigeration not occurred, Green (along with company founder Joseph Thompson) could have been content in the Zone of Status Quo delivering ice. But the disruption forced them into the Zone of Adoption, and that adoption led to a curiosity that bore fruit in the Zone of Innovation. Which means, the next time you're enjoying a Slurpee, you should consider its simple origins as a one-time block of ice. The good news for leaders is that the innovation didn't start with a mandate to reinvent their business or disrupt the grocery-store market, but as a desire to extend the existing change curve a bit further than before.

The Zone of Innovation is where the cost of change can yield an ever greater payoff. And while it's tempting to plant a flag and declare victory as you exit the Zone of Adoption and get back to the results you had reached before, in many cases, there's a bigger win to be had.

Reactions in the Zone of Innovation

In *Who Rocked the Boat?*, the captain and crew managed to get *Results* back to the status quo. But the unexpected change produced a change in them as well. The captain took the opportunity to celebrate how each crew member contributed to their success:

> *"Say what you will, but we've overcome a lot to get to this point,"* the captain said. *"And hey, it took everyone working together."*
>
> The captain then turned to each of the crew members in turn: *"Move, you're never stuck in the old way of doing things. I can always count on you to try something new. And Minimize, I love how you always focus on what's necessary so we don't get in over our heads. Wait, you ask the best questions, and you don't rush headlong into things. Resist, you force us to test our thinking, which is invaluable. And Quit, even when you're disengaged, I've learned you can be an early warning signal to something the rest of us may not be seeing. What an amazing crew you are!*

The captain wasn't just offering compliments for compliments' sake. It was a reminder of the crew's capacity to work together and overcome difficult challenges. As a leader, the captain made it safe for the crew to be curious about what else they might do.

"I love the creativity," the captain said, "but Resist *has a point—the river has some natural limitations. I wonder if there's a way to get off the river...?"*

Not all the ideas were necessarily productive (*Quit* suggested abandoning the cargo), but the captain had made it safe enough for the crew to explore possibilities and activated the crew's participation in the Zone of Innovation. The captain was also able to nudge them toward a solution, not by jumping in with an answer, but by asking a directed question: "Is there a way to get off the river?"

Innovation takes work, and the Zone of Innovation isn't without obstacles to overcome. As the Southland Ice Company shifted to the refrigeration business and turned their warehouses into convenience stores, they had to learn about traffic patterns around their locations, refine their marketing, and track which products were worth keeping on the shelves and which were not.[31] Such innovation requires an ongoing sense of curiosity and optimism.

Captain's Corner

Unpacking the Change Experience

Because the Zone of Innovation benefits from reflection on the change journey to this point, take time to explore the insights, motivation, and experiences of your team. Consider holding a team meeting and asking:

- What tools, processes, or functions did we use in unique ways while going through the Zone of Adoption?
- What did we stop doing in the Zone of Adoption that could be a model for other stuff to which we could say no?
- What obstacles did we work around, and how can we apply those workarounds to other areas?
- Where did we lose people along the change journey?
    - What led them to give up and/or quit?
    - Can we address some of that as part of our innovation?

- Where were we able to strengthen our relationships with each other and with others, both inside and outside the organization?
  - How can we leverage those improved relationships?
- How can we take the negative reptilian-brain reactions out of our future work and create more of the positive reactions that enable innovation?

Shauna Smith and Four Foods Group

In the last chapter, we saw how Shauna Smith, her leadership team, and her restaurant employees were engaged and resourceful. They came up with ways to pull themselves out of the Zone of Adoption with happy customers and revived and thriving brands. But they weren't done yet—they had new insights into their capabilities and what might be next.

If you recall, they helped their employees feel safe and cared for when coming to work by doing things like providing meal packs for employees and their families. But their needs extended to other necessary staples, like toilet paper and milk. Smith and her team created "family packs" with the additional essentials included. "Then we let them know that every time they came to work, we'd give them a family pack to take home," Smith later recounted.

It would have been easy to stop there. But because Smith and her leaders had built a culture that encouraged team members to stay curious, one eventually asked: "Why don't we sell these family packs to customers?" And suddenly, it was obvious: other families were facing the same challenges and would happily pay for the solution. That sense of curiosity, tied to a change that is already occurring, is what the Zone of Innovation is all about.

Sharing the Stories of Change

A leader can invite additional curiosity in the Zone of Innovation by sharing their team's own stories about going through the change together. Such stories can have tremendous benefits:

- They make it safe for team members to share their individual insights about going through the change so that the rest of the team can benefit.
- They provide a safe method of feedback to help the leader understand

what they may have missed, where they fell short, or what worked well.

- They allow the team to see themselves as the "heroes" in the story as they overcame obstacles and challenges together.
- They fuel motivation as the team recognizes they're getting better at change.
- They establish the undergirding for a "change culture," shifting the starting mindset from an assumption that change is a negative to one in which change is an opportunity to stretch themselves and realize greater success.

As we referenced previously, stories are powerful. Take advantage of your time in the Zone of Innovation to pause and talk about the stories of your adventure, as the captain and crew did in *Who Rocked the Boat?* As Angela Rodriguez, an expert in culturally driven marketing, said: "Storytelling is at the core of culture. It is how histories are passed down, how customs are shared, and how traditions become endemic to a group. Shared culture is rooted in a shared tradition of communicating. The stories a group tells communicate what a culture values."[32] And let's be honest, it feels good to be on a winning team, to escape the victim mindset so tempting in the Zone of Disruption, and to become a change champion. Building a culture of change success in the Zone of Innovation further prepares you and your team for the next waterfall ahead.

Building a culture of change success in the Zone of Innovation further prepares you and your team for the next waterfall ahead.

Build on the Momentum and Leverage of Change

Moving through the Change Model holds advantages for the kind of connected innovation we're talking about in the Zone of Innovation. For the Southland Ice Company, it was taking their existing storefronts and filling them with groceries instead of ice. For Shauna Smith and Four Foods Group, it was repurposing a stopgap employee solution—"family packs"—and selling them to their existing patrons. Each was made possible by the existing change muscle and momentum gained, along with a newfound sense of curiosity.

Let's visualize this "muscle and momentum" as a lever with "innovation" represented as a block on the far end. Without passing through the Zone of Disruption and the ascent up the Zone of Adoption, innovation often looks like this:

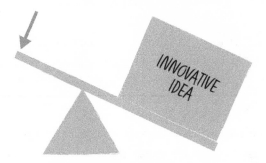

FIGURE 40: *Trying to Lift an Idea Without Much Leverage.*

It takes a significant amount of creative thinking and force to lift the innovative idea off the ground. Yet, because of the change—with its difficult climb inspired by effective leadership—we extend the "lever" as the team's momentum and change muscle increases. Now, in the Zone of Innovation, a leader's invitation to be curious and have their team explore "What else?" requires much less creative force to bring the innovation to life.

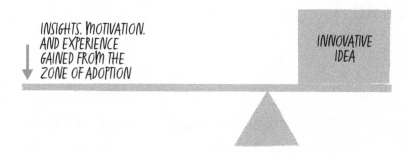

FIGURE 41: *Innovating Is Easier With Leverage Gained in the Zone of Adoption.*

Invite, Don't Stifle, Curiosity

After traveling the squiggly line in the Zone of Adoption, trying things, hitting dead ends, struggling, and trying again, you and your team are no strangers to asking, "What else...?" You've grown accustomed to learning from what doesn't work. And frankly, having gotten out of the dip, you're probably pretty good at it by now.

Arriving in the Zone of Innovation, you know your team members better than you did before (being in the trenches with your people during tough struggles teaches you a lot about how they each react to change); you know better what motivates them, inspires them, and engages them. As you've shared the story of change together, you know their strengths and they know yours. Now you are primed to invite further curiosity around the powerful Zone of Innovation question "What else...?"

Captain's Corner

Invite Directed Curiosity and Exploration

As a leader, use the Zone of Innovation to instill a sense of curiosity in your team. We use the word "directed" to highlight that you're extending an invitation to be curious and explore new ideas as they relate to the change—not a free-for-all exploration of any and all things that might fall under an "innovation" rubric. Help your team focus on what else they can do to extend the change trajectory and rise above the previous status quo. Consider the suggestions below for building an innovation culture in your team.

Engage in open-ended conversations that help your team members explore opportunities made possible by the change:

- Debrief your Zone of Adoption experiences by asking:
  - Were there unintended outcomes from the change?
  - How could we minimize or maximize those outcomes?
  - If we had to start over again, what would we do?
- Expand a sense of what's possible by asking:
  - Who benefits from the change now?
  - Who else could benefit?
  - How?
  - What opportunities can we see now that we didn't see before?
  - What could make the change even more valuable?
  - What else could we do?

Celebrating Your Way to Innovation

On May 23, 2019, Dolores Al Shelleh reached the summit of Mount Everest, and became the first Jordanian woman to do so. Of that experience, she said, "Reaching the top is a feeling that I will never forget. I felt most alive, I felt most human, and I felt how important it is to connect to each other to build up the teamwork together, to care about the others on the summit. And that's how I started searching more about what can I take on next."[33]

Dolores was celebrating her and her team's success. Notice the order of what Dolores felt at the summit: she first noticed her own reactions as feeling "most alive" and "most human." She then recognized their success was made possible by her team's connectedness, how they worked together, and how they had grown to care about each other. And finally, she considered how these things led to her asking, "What can I take on next?"

Celebrating on the top of Everest was, of necessity, simple—a few selfies, hugs, and pats on the back. We'd guess taking a moment and enjoying the intrinsic rewards of her accomplishment were more profound and memorable. Which begs the question for leaders: How should you and your team celebrate your own successful summit out of the Zone of Adoption? Not lacking daylight or oxygen, you likely have more options. But the key is understanding how your team members *want* to celebrate and be recognized. Some people are good with the intrinsic—to pause and look over their accomplishment and think, *We did that!* For others, eating cake together in the break room and sharing their accomplishments would be perfect. Either way, effective change leaders don't shrug off the opportunity to celebrate with their teams. Instead, they recognize it as a key element in the Zone of Innovation. Such moments of recognition, expressed intrinsically or extrinsically, can strengthen the bonds of a team and turn their attention to "What else could we do?"

Marché Pleshette

Bringing Introspection Into Your Celebration

The Zone of Innovation isn't just about celebrating success, but also growth, possibilities, and preparedness. It's the recognition of an expansion of opportunities to do things you could not have done, or maybe never even considered doing, before.

Getting to the Zone of Innovation indicates a lot about

a team's capacity to be the difference—and that is not to be under-estimated. As we have explored the dynamics of change, we know change can be one of the most feared and resisted experiences, as it takes us from a place of comfort into potentially uncharted territory. It takes hard work! In the Zone of Innovation, we've strengthened our team's capacity to shift their minds, actions, and routines right along with circumstantial changes. It's an enlightening experience. In fact, the Zone of Innovation could be seen as a zone of elevated empowerment. It's the evidence that we could, we did, and that it's possible... whatever "it" may be. And we should celebrate that and reward ourselves.

Research shows that the best rewards are usually intrinsic—the satisfaction we have in doing something. Doing that difficult thing is a reward in itself. But don't ignore the extrinsic—like buying lunch for your team, handing out theater tickets, or anything else your team members would find rewarding and motivating. Such extrinsic rewards can lift you and others—to a point. Research also shows that, if not handled well, the bonuses, gift certificates, and even raises in salary can become demotivators. Studies with children have shown well-intentioned extrinsic reward strategies can backfire and undermine internal motivation.

If your team really likes extrinsic rewards, consider using partial reinforcement and vary how and when you offer rewards (for more on this, read Alfie Kohn's book *Punished by Rewards*). So be careful with extrinsic rewards. The feeling of a job well done is often motivation enough. Emphasize the intrinsic as you reward those you lead. Celebrate small wins along the way, and high-five yourself when you emerge on the other side of change.

Further, take the time in the Zone of Innovation to consider how you've all grown together—practically, intellectually, and personally. Honor the good, the bad, and the ugly in how you have learned to navigate and relate to change, because it's all in service to growth.

Rather than put a period on the end of the Innovation experience, place ellipses. Celebrate and introspect. Honor your awesome capacity to create greatness! Innovation has everything to do with maximizing the change experience, multiplying its benefits, and being prepared for the inevitable change that will come again. Knowing and doing this distinguishes you as an outstanding navigator of change and a realizer of exponential results!

Captain's Corner

Celebrate Your Success

Be intentional in the Zone of Innovation to celebrate success with your team. The very fact that you've made it to this zone is an achievement worthy of pausing and celebrating! Ask yourself:

- Based on the stories we've shared as a team, what were the milestones or individual achievements that most stand out?
- How do such achievements connect to the strategy, objectives, or values of the organization? (It's not necessary that they do, but worth pointing out if you can show the alignment).
- Consider the personalities and culture of your team. Are they more intrinsically or extrinsically motivated?
- Based on the above, what can you do as a celebration of success that rewards individuals and your team in the way they want to receive recognition and praise?

From the Zone of Innovation to a New River Routine

Leaving the Zone of Innovation, even with higher results, means eventually finding your way back to the River Routine. But because you've used a framework that's given your team a common way of talking about and experiencing change, there's something different. The river will always run its natural course, but your crew has become better at navigating its length. That benefits everyone on the good ship *Results* as you and those you lead prepare for the next inevitable waterfall.

Conclusion

The international phone provider Three was sitting in a comfortable Zone of Status Quo. They'd experienced consistent (if relatively small) growth during the previous years, and they were providing good (not great) customer service. However, they weren't satisfied. They wanted to become number one and, after much discussion, they decided they wanted to win the highly coveted J.D. Power Award (a quality award based on customer surveys).

Of course, they knew they couldn't achieve that kind of success without change. After all, what they had done previously had only gotten them so far along the River Routine. To achieve greatness, they'd need to update a few things around the office (and not just the coffee machine in the break room).

This is where change leaders came into play. After hearing about their goals and aspirations, change leaders met with management to walk them through the Change Model. They painted a vision for their leaders—showed them the flow of the river, how to look for waterfalls, and how to size up the steep cliff. This not only established the *why* of the change, but also gave valuable insights on where they were coming from and how to get to where they wanted to go. To make sure all their teams were on the same page, executives published the change vision so everyone in the company could see it and jump on board. And not a moment too soon. After the necessary preparations were made, management bid a final farewell to the Zone of Status Quo and leaped over the waterfall.

As Three's version of the ship *Results* plummeted to the ravine below, management had the crew well prepared. Training launched as they entered the Zone of Disruption—training that came at all levels, from those on the call floor dealing with customers to high-level managers running entire branches or regions. Everyone was meant to move together, and the training helped the company understand what was happening and what was expected of them throughout the change journey. As a result, employees were continuously informed about the *why* and the *how*.

The training worked wonders, and before they knew it, Three was in the Zone of Adoption. Time to try some new things.

Three's executives focused on a handful of major points of improvement (what FranklinCovey refers to as Wildly Important Goals) during this time: (1) revitalizing communication, (2) building more capability in team leaders leading change, and (3) decreasing call-center turnover.

One of their biggest changes came in the form of recognition. As they swirled through the trial-and-error path up the Zone of Adoption, they checked data on how, when, and where they were improving. Rather than hanging their heads at any losses (which they accounted for in their change vision), Three watched for improvements. Any employee that showed they could handle customer service better, faster, and with a higher customer-satisfaction score, would be recognized, rewarded, and their best practices adopted by their coworkers. By doing so, any wins were multiplied across the customer-service floor.

And while much of this may seem straightforward and simple, there were plenty of hiccups, missteps, and struggles along the way. But because Three was anticipating the change and prepared for it, they innovated and experienced growth relatively quickly.

And yes, in addition to realizing significant financial improvements, they also won the J.D. Power Award.

Three is a good example of an organization traveling the length of the Change Model—a model you've now invested some time getting familiar with. But keep in mind, as George Box, one of the great statistical minds of the twentieth century, said: "Now it would be very remarkable if any system existing in the real world could be exactly represented by any simple model.... For such a model there is no need to ask if the model is 'true.' If 'truth' is to be the 'whole truth' the answer must be 'No.' The only question of interest is 'Is the model illuminating and useful?'"[34]

Yes, you will find those rare exceptions when an organization jumps the chasm or has a smooth journey up the cliff. Yet, even with such outliers, our experience is that the Change Model is both illuminating and useful—whether as a map, a compass, or both. We also know such a shared framework can build a positive change culture within your team and even organization. As fellow FranklinCovey author Todd Davis writes in his bestselling book *Get Better: 15 Proven Practices to Build Effective Relationships at Work*, "You've probably heard the adage that an organization's greatest assets are its people. I'd like to take that one step further and share that, in my experience, it's the relationships between those people that...become an organization's ultimate competitive advantage."[35]

A remarkable benefit that can come from change, even when that change is unexpected or unwanted, is the opportunity to strengthen the relationships around you. And with such a "competitive advantage," such teams are more successful when taking on the next change, and the next... because the Change Model never ends. The path through the Zone of Innovation eventually becomes a new Zone of Status Quo, leading to a new Zone of Disruption and unique Zone of Adoption climb. The change river is ever flowing, with the change waterfall a constant feature—sometimes anticipated, sometimes steered toward, but often unexpected. Yet, wise leaders/captains understand that *how* they lead through today's change shapes the outcomes of the next change around the bend—for good or bad. So we invite you to keep this book handy and refer to the Captain's Corners often (audio listeners can download them as a PDF) as you lead your team through the change journey. By doing so, we know that the inherent disruption and uncertainty can be turned into the opportunity to envision more, achieve more, and *become* more.

And really, that's what change is all about.

Acknowledgments

Curtis Bateman

Perhaps you're like me when you see a book with an author's name on it—you don't think much about it. As a new author, I have a newfound appreciation for the village involved in writing and publishing a book, and I want to gratefully acknowledge the many who have been part of this project.

Curt Garbett and Peter Miller. My two former business partners, friends, and collaborators for many years while together we developed and tested the early thinking for the Change Model.

FranklinCovey and the book team. Amazing expertise and experience. I have tremendous gratitude to them for guiding and managing this project. Thank you, Scott Miller, Annie Oswald, and Zach Kristensen. And to Platte Clark, Brian Johnson, and his team, who have been amazing thought partners, writers, and researchers. Platte may have redefined the word "patience" helping us on this journey. And our illustrator and book designer, Lauren Ball. From the very start he 'got it' and created the amazing artwork and book layout.

I feel significant gratitude to my coauthors Marché Pleschette, Christi Phillips, and Andy Cindrich. Together, we have debated, collaborated, and created a leadership book on change. Along that journey, the parable emerged as a way to teach and share some of our key learnings. They graciously allowed me to branch off and follow a passion for parables that I developed while collaborating for nearly ten years with Dr. Spencer Johnson, author of *Who Moved My Cheese?*

Most importantly to my wife, Elaine, who never faltered in her support as I spent countless extra hours hidden away in my office writing, Zoom calling, debating, creating, and working to share this topic of change which has captivated me for over twenty years.

Marché Pleshette

I express a debt of gratitude to Scott Miller for having always seen the greatness in me and for giving me the opportunity to realize an aspect of that as an author. Your brilliance speaks for itself, but you are an even greater human being than the world may know.

My coauthors and book-development team—Curtis Bateman, Andy Cindrich, Christi Phillips, Platte Clark, and Brian Johnson—you have all felt beautifully familiar from the start. I've upped my understanding of synergy through our many conversations and processes where every person was valued, every idea considered, and the blend of it all allowed us to materialize a book to help others process through life's promised experience of consistent change!

My beautiful mom, Zoie Thompson, has shown me that the change that happens as we age happens also with those who love us through the aging process. The accolades you gave me whenever I read drafts of my writing never got old. You are my personal cheerleader and best friend.

I am tremendously grateful to the executives at FranklinCovey who gave a thumbs-up when my name was considered for this project. I can truly say at FranklinCovey I am a valued member of a winning team, doing meaningful work, in an environment of trust.

Andy Cindrich

It's been a dream come true to be involved in this project. I'm grateful to Scott Miller for a career's worth of not-so-gentle prodding to prepare myself for this opportunity. The "My dog has more followers than you on LinkedIn" early-morning text is probably most memorable.

I'm grateful to be partnered with Curtis Bateman, Marché Pleshette, and Christi Phillips on this project, and to have seen the power of synergy manifest in real time on our numerous weekly author calls.

I'm not sure this book could have happened without the expertise, guidance, and polish of three gentlemen who will individually swear, "I was never here!" at the book launch party. Platte Clark, Brian Johnson, and Logan Davis have been delightful to work with.

Thanks to our author coach Zach Kristensen and our head coach Annie Oswald for their patient persistence, wisdom, and expert guidance.

Finally, thanks to my beautiful wife, Suzie, for never begrudging a minute I've spent on this book or on any of the things I do to try and make a difference in the world.

Christi Phillips

I have deep gratitude for Todd Davis, who heard, during our first Contribution Conversation of my first year at FranklinCovey, that I hoped to write for FranklinCovey one day. I was thinking maybe after I'd made my fifth or tenth work anniversary. But just ten months later, I'm falling over my self-fulfilling-prophesied waterfall because Todd was actively listening.

I'm grateful to Curtis Bateman, Marché Pleshette, and Andy Cindrich for welcoming me to this solid authoring team with joy and collaboration. Talk about getting into someone else's boat!

Thank you to Platte Clark, Brian Johnson, and Logan Davis for making it impossible for me to fail and for your expertise and creativity. And to Scott Miller and Annie Oswald, for the invitation to join the standard bearers of the brand we all love.

Author Bios

Curtis Bateman is FranklinCovey's vice president of international direct offices, with over twenty-five years of experience in the training industry. His passion for enabling organizations "at change" resulted in the co-creation of transformative, industry-leading solutions, including Change Element, Leaders@Change, Managing Millennials, Millennials@Work, and the Change Practitioner.

Connect with Curtis.

LinkedIn: www.linkedin.com/in/curtisabateman
Instagram: www.instagram.com/curtisabateman/

Marché Pleshette is a skilled leadership coach who has been a FranklinCovey consultant for fifteen years. She has been the subject-matter expert for *The 7 Habits of Highly Effective People* and serves on FranklinCovey's consultant coaching team, ensuring the quality of their world-class consultants. She holds a bachelor's degree in mass communications, is certified through the International Coach Federation, and has been trained through the Hudson Institute of Coaching.

Connect with Marché.

LinkedIn: www.linkedin.com/in/marchepleshette/

Andy Cindrich is a FranklinCovey senior consultant whose personal mission statement is to help teams and individuals win. Andy played a key role in developing FranklinCovey's *The 4 Disciplines of Execution* solution, which has helped clients all over the world achieve breakthrough results. He has a master's in educational leadership, a bachelor's degree in teaching both psychology and history, and a minor in coaching.

Connect with Andy.

LinkedIn: www.linkedin.com/in/cindrich/

Instagram: www.instagram.com/cindrich/

Twitter: www.twitter.com/cindrich

YouTube: www.youtube.com/channel/UCWwXzIA4kqGQj8MobBdZX6Q

Christi Phillips is FranklinCovey's director of learning, development, and inclusion. She has also served as a developmental consultant, program developer, and talent coach. Christi has a PhD in human resource development from Texas A&M University, a master's in business management, and bachelor's degrees in political science and French.

Connect with Christi.

LinkedIn: www.linkedin.com/in/christi-phillips-ph-d-259b276/

Google Scholar: scholar.google.com/citations?user=Tz_xrEYAAAAJ&hl=en

Endnotes

1   Cost, Ben, and Nadine DeNinno. "Why Charlie Watts Once Punched Mick Jagger in His Rude Rock Star Face." *New York Post*, August 25, 2021. nypost.com/2021/08/24/why-charlie-watts-once-punched-mick-jagger-in-the-face.

Edison, Mike. " 'Never Call Me Your Drummer Again'—The Full Story of the Time Charlie Watts Punched Mick Jagger, excerpted from *Sympathy for the Drummer.*" *Vulture*, New York, August 25, 2021. www.vulture.com/article/book-excerpt-rolling-stones-charlie-watts-mick-jagger-fight.html.

Petridis, Alexis. "Charlie Watts: The Calm, Brilliant Eye of the Rolling Stones' Rock'n'Roll Storm." *The Guardian*, August 24, 2021. www.theguardian.com/music/2021/aug/24/charlie-watts-the-calm-brilliant-eye-of-the-rolling-stones-rocknroll-storm.

2   Malone, Erin D. "The Kubler-Ross change curve and the flipped classroom: Moving students past the pit of despair." *Education in the Health Professions Journal*, 2018; 1:36–40.

3   Schwartz, H., ed. *Imperial Messages: One Hundred Modern Parables*. Overlook Press, 1991.

4   "About Us." Illuminati Labs. www.illuminatilabs.com/about-us.

5   Gottlich, Max. "NFT Market Tops $40B in 2021 Amid Growing Interest." Seeking Alpha, January 6, 2022. seekingalpha.com/news/3785928-nft-market-tops-40b-in-2021-amid-growing-interest-bloomberg.

6   Asher-Schapiro, Avi. "Hundreds of Salesforce Employees Object to NFT Plans." *Context*, February 18, 2022. news.trust.org/item/20220218170402-ug6bk.

7   Leonard, David, and Claude Coltea. "Most Change Initiatives Fail—But They Don't Have To." *Gallup Business Journal*, May 24, 2013. news.gallup.com/businessjournal/162707/change-initiatives-fail-don.aspx.

8   Kounang, Nadia. "What Is the Science Behind Fear?" CNN Health, October 29, 2015. www.cnn.com/2015/10/29/health/science-of-fear.

9   Miner, John B. "Consultants Employed by McKinsey & Company." *Organizational Behavior* 5, 2008, 77–82. doi.org/10.4324/9781315701974-15.

10 Bayiz, Ahmad, and Zhichao Cheng. "The Role of Change Content, Context, Process, and Leadership in Understanding Employees' Commitment to Change: The Case of Public Organizations in Kurdistan Region of Iraq." *Public Personnel Management* 47, no. 2 (2018): 195–216. doi.org/10.1177/0091026017753645.

11 Arnéguy, Elodie, Marc Ohana, and Florence Stinglhamber. "Organizational Justice and Readiness for Change: A Concomitant Examination of the Mediating Role of Perceived Organizational Support and Identification." *Frontiers in Psychology* 9 (2018). doi.org/10.3389/fpsyg.2018.01172.

12 Brown, Brené. "How to Identify Your Negative Emotions: The Happiness Lab with Dr. Laurie Santos." Pushkin Industries, May 9, 2022. www.pushkin.fm/podcasts/the-happiness-lab-with-dr-laurie-santos/how-to-identify-your-negative-emotions.

13 Sinek, Simon. *Start with Why: How Great Leaders Inspire Everyone to Take Action.* London: Penguin Books Ltd, 2011.

14 "Where Basketball Was Invented: The History of Basketball." Springfield College. springfield.edu/where-basketball-was-invented-the-birthplace-of-basketball.

15 "James Naismith's Life and Legacy: Celebrating 150 Years." The University of Kansas. exhibits.lib.ku.edu/exhibits/show/naismith150/collections/radio-interview.

16 "Study: The Risks of Ignoring Employee Feedback." *Leadership IQ*, March 10, 2022. https://www.leadershipiq.com/blogs/leadershipiq/study-the-risks-of-ignoring-employee-feedback.

17 "When Chagall and Malraux Shook up the Palais Garnier Opera House." *Opera Online*, September 23, 2014. www.opera-online.com/en/articles/when-chagall-and-malraux-shook-up-the-palais-garnier-opera-house.

18 "How likely are you to have an animal collision?" State Farm. www.statefarm.com/simple-insights/auto-and-vehicles/how-likely-are-you-to-have-an-animal-collision.

19 McGrath, R. G. *Seeing Around Corners: How to Spot Inflection Points in Business Before They Happen.* Mariner Books, 2021.

20 Pradhan, Sudeepta, and Ranajee Ranajee. "Turnaround to Transformation: The case of Thermax." Conference: XVI Annual Convention of Strategic Management Forum: India & Indigenous strategies. At: Kozhikode. May 2013, www.researchgate.net/publication/301886961_Turnaround_to_Transformation_The_case_of_Thermax.

21 "How a shareholder's letter to Anu Aga catalysed change at Thermax." ET Bureau, *The Economic Times*, October 5, 2012. economictimes.indiatimes.com/how-a-shareholders-letter-to-anu-aga-catalysed-change-at-thermax/articleshow/16669747.cms.

22 Perry, B. P. "The Japanese Soldier Who Kept on Fighting after WW2 Had Finished." Sky HISTORY TV Channel, www.history.co.uk/shows/lost-gold-of-wwii/articles/the-japanese-soldier-who-kept-on-fighting-after-ww2-had-finished.

23 Pitogo, Heziel. "Remembering Hiroo Onoda: Japanese Soldier Who Fought WWII for 29 Years After It Ended!" WAR HISTORY ONLINE, April 22, 2015. www.warhistoryonline.com/war-articles/hiroo-onoda-japanese-soldier-who-fought-wwii-for-29-years-after-it-ended.html.

24   "Escape Room." Wikipedia. en.wikipedia.org/wiki/Escape_room.

25   King, R. "More than 110,000 eating and drinking establishments closed in 2020." *Fortune*, January 26, 2021. fortune.com/2021/01/26/restaurants-bars-closed-2020-jobs-lost-how-many-have-closed-us-covid-pandemic-stimulus-unemployment.

26   Wiseman, Liz. *Multipliers: How the Best Leaders Make Everyone Smarter.* New York, NY: HarperBusiness, an imprint of HarperCollinsPublishers, 2017.

27   Erin, Marc D, Bt, Sarah McIntosh, Boston379, Lb, Sr, Cay, Section E - anonymous, and Carolina Perry. "Submissions Archive - Page 132 of 464." Technology and Operations Management, November 15, 2017. https://digital.hbs.edu/platform-rctom/submission/page/132/.

28   "Siemens to establish mobile working as core component of the 'new normal' " Siemens. July 16, 2020. press.siemens.com/global/en/pressrelease/siemens-establish-mobile-working-core-component-new-normal.

29   Tippett, Ben. "The Complete Guide to Understanding Rugby." Deadspin, June 26, 2017. deadspin.com/the-complete-guide-to-understanding-rugby-1796388722.

30   "7-Eleven is 70,000 Stores Strong." Cision PR Newswire. January 23, 2020. www.prnewswire.com/news-releases/7-eleven-is-70-000-stores-strong-300992154.html.

31   "The Southland Corporation." Encyclopedia.com. May 23, 2018. www.encyclopedia.com/social-sciences-and-law/economics-business-and-labor/businesses-and-occupations/southland-corp.

32   Mizrahi, I., and A. Rodriguez. "Storytelling Is a Different Story for Each Culture." *Forbes*, February 19, 2019. www.forbes.com/sites/isaacmizrahi/2019/02/19/storytelling-is-a-different-story-for-each-culture.

33   EuroNews. "Meet the first Jordanian woman to climb Mount Everest." YouTube. August 15, 2022. www.youtube.com/watch?v=GnZ9UdEujrk&t=144s.

34   Box, G. E. P. "Robustness in the strategy of scientific model building." *Robustness in Statistics*, edited by R. L. Launer and G. N. Wilkinson, 201–236., Academic Press, 1979, doi:10.1016/B978-0-12-438150-6.50018-2.

35   Davis, T. *Get Better: 15 Proven Practices to Build Effective Relationships at Work.* Introduction, Simon & Schuster, 2019.

FranklinCovey is the most trusted leadership company in the world, with operations in over 160 countries. We transform organizations by partnering with our clients to build leaders, teams, and cultures that get breakthrough results through collective action, which leads to a more engaging work experience for their people.

Available through the FranklinCovey All Access Pass®, our best-in-class content, solutions, experts, technology, and metrics seamlessly integrate to ensure lasting behavior change at scale.

This approach to leadership and organizational change has been tested and refined by working with tens of thousands of teams and organizations over the past 35 years.

To learn more, visit
FRANKLINCOVEY.COM

SCHEDULE A SPEAKER
FOR YOUR NEXT EVENT

CURTIS BATEMAN   MARCHÉ PLESHETTE   ANDY CINDRICH   CHRISTI PHILLIPS, PH.D.

Are you planning an event for your organization? Schedule one of the authors of *Change: How to Turn Uncertainty Into Opportunity* to deliver an engaging keynote or work session tailored to your leaders or audience.

- Association and Industry Conferences
- Sales Conferences
- Annual Meetings
- Leadership Development

- Executive and Board Retreats
- Company Functions
- Onsite Consulting
- Client Engagements

These experts have spoken at hundreds of conferences and client events worldwide.

To schedule a speaker today, call
1-888-554-1776
or visit **franklincovey.com/speakers-bureau**

All Access Pass

The FranklinCovey All Access Pass® provides unlimited access to our best-in-class content and solutions, allowing you to expand your reach, achieve your business objectives, and sustainably impact performance across your organization.

AS A PASSHOLDER, YOU CAN:

- Access FranklinCovey's world-class content, whenever and wherever you need it, including *The 7 Habits of Highly Effective People®: Signature Edition 4.0*, Leading at the *Speed of Trust®*, *The 5 Choices to Extraordinary Productivity®*, and *Unconscious Bias: Understanding Bias to Unleash Potential™*.

- Certify your internal facilitators to teach our content, deploy FranklinCovey consultants, or use digital content to reach your learners with the behavior-changing content you require.

- Have access to a certified implementation specialist who will help design Impact Journeys for behavior change.

- Organize FranklinCovey content around your specific business-related needs.

- Build a common learning experience throughout your entire global organization with our core-content areas localized into 24 languages.

Join thousands of organizations using the All Access Pass to implement strategy, close operational gaps, increase sales, drive customer loyalty, and improve employee engagement.

To learn more, visit
FRANKLINCOVEY.COM or call **1-888-868-1776**

CHANGE
How to Turn Uncertainty Into Opportunity ™

FranklinCovey
ALL ACCESS PASS

Change happens all the time, whether we choose it or it chooses us.

Yet, when faced with change, many organizations primarily focus on the process. Successful change takes more than that—**it's your people who make change happen**. And as people, we're wired to react to change to survive, which can make change feel difficult or threatening. Successful leaders engage their people in change, making it feel less uncertain and more like an opportunity.

Introducing *Change: How to Turn Uncertainty Into Opportunity*

When we recognize that change follows a predictable pattern, we can learn to manage our reactions and understand how to navigate change, both functionally and emotionally. This allows us to consciously determine how to best move forward—even in the most challenging stages.

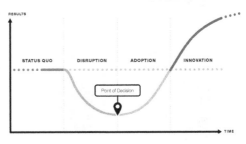

Change: How to Turn Uncertainty Into Opportunity helps individuals and leaders learn how to successfully navigate any workplace change to improve results.

To learn more about how FranklinCovey's
Change: How to Turn Uncertainty Into Opportunity
can support your team and organization, visit

franklincovey.com/leadership/navigate-change

 **FranklinCovey**™

Read More
FROM THE FRANKLINCOVEY LIBRARY

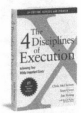

MORE THAN 50 MILLION COPIES SOLD

Learn more about how to develop yourself personally, lead your team, or transform your organization with these bestselling books, by visiting **7habitsstore.com**.

FRANKLINCOVEY
ONLEADERSHIP
WITH
SCOTT MILLER

Join *On Leadership* host Scott Miller for weekly interviews with thought leaders, bestselling authors, and world-renowned experts on the topics of organizational culture, leadership development, execution, and personal productivity.

FEATURED INTERVIEWS INCLUDE:

CHRIS McCHESNEY
THE 4 DISCIPLINES OF EXECUTION

SUSAN DAVID
EMOTIONAL AGILITY

KIM SCOTT
RADICAL CANDOR

DANIEL PINK
WHEN

SETH GODIN
THE DIP, LINCHPIN, PURPLE COW

NELY GALÁN
SELF MADE

LIZ WISEMAN
MULTIPLIERS

GUY KAWASAKI
WISE GUY

STEPHEN M. R. COVEY
THE SPEED OF TRUST

ARIANNA HUFFINGTON
THRIVE NOW

NANCY DUARTE
DATA STORY, SLIDE:OLOGY

STEPHANIE McMAHON
CHIEF BRAND OFFICER, WWE

DEEPAK CHOPRA
ABUNDANCE

ANNE CHOW
CEO, AT&T BUSINESS

GENERAL STANLEY McCHRYSTAL
LEADERS: MYTH AND REALITY

MATTHEW McCONAUGHEY
GREENLIGHTS

Subscribe to FranklinCovey's *On Leadership* to receive weekly videos, tools, articles, and podcasts at

FRANKLINCOVEY.COM/ONLEADERSHIP

Mango Publishing, established in 2014, publishes an eclectic list of books by diverse authors—both new and established voices—on topics ranging from business, personal growth, women's empowerment, LGBTQ+ studies, health, and spirituality to history, popular culture, time management, decluttering, lifestyle, mental wellness, aging, and sustainable living. We were named 2019 *and* 2020's #1 fastest-growing independent publisher by *Publishers Weekly*. Our success is driven by our main goal, which is to publish high-quality books that will entertain readers as well as make a positive difference in their lives.

Our readers are our most important resource; we value your input, suggestions, and ideas. We'd love to hear from you—after all, we are publishing books for you!

Please stay in touch with us and follow us at:

Facebook: Mango Publishing
Twitter: @MangoPublishing
Instagram: @MangoPublishing
LinkedIn: Mango Publishing
Pinterest: Mango Publishing
Newsletter: mangopublishinggroup.com/newsletter

Join us on Mango's journey to reinvent publishing, one book at a time.

CPSIA information can be obtained
at www.ICGtesting.com
Printed in the USA
JSHW022132230423
40694JS00001B/1